Not There

MARIUSZ SZCZYGIEŁ

Translated from the Polish with an Afterword
by Antonia Lloyd-Jones

Linden Editions

Linden Editions, 110 Standen Rd, London SW18 5TS
www.lindeneditions.com

This English language edition published in the UK in 2025 by Linden Editions

First published by Dowody na Istnienie in Poland in Warsaw, 2018, with the title *Nie ma*

9 8 7 6 5 4 3 2 1

ISBN: 978-1-0687404-8-0
eISBN: 978-1-0687404-9-7

A CIP catalogue record for this book is available from the British Library

Cover image © Maria Norek
Cover design © Tasja Pulawska

Text design and typesetting by Tetragon, London
Printed in England by TJ Books, Padstow, Cornwall

This publication has been supported by the ©POLAND Translation Programme

EU Authorised Representative: Easy Access System Europe – Mustamäe tee 50, 10621 Tallinn, Estonia, gpsr.requests@easproject.com.

Nothing in this book is made up.
If I'd made it up it would have been much more interesting.

Contents

Not There

Not There

DEDICATION

Since I first started collecting material for this book in 2009 – with intervals lasting several years, I'm sorry to say – a number of my close friends have died. I had talked to most of them about my work on *Not There*. There were some I hadn't told about it, but I wanted to present copies of the book to all of them once it was published.

I dedicate *Not There* to them.

They are:

Elżbieta Bednarkiewicz
Maciej Firlej
Viola Fischerová
Krystyna Goldbergowa
Joanna Hornik-Grabowiecka
Kora
Lidia Ostałowska
Iwona Ostapkowicz
Gayga
Tomasz Stańko
Leonard Talmont
Teresa Torańska

and Zofia Czerwińska, who died after this book was first
published.

They keep turning up, uninvited, more and more of them. They
like to come via email or Messenger. And the older I get, the
more they multiply.

He/She has died.

Whenever I get one of these messages, I think, 'That's
another one who's coming to live with me now.'

When Iwona Ostapkowicz joined the list above, this is
what I wrote to her niece: 'I remember the time my friend and
I invited her to supper. Now they're both gone... I wonder if
their consciousness is floating around somewhere? But I'm
afraid our consciousness fizzles out if there's no brain chemistry
to keep it alive. They can only go on living in our memory – and
they will. So Iwona is coming to live with me too.'

They keep turning up, uninvited, more and more of them.
They like to come via email or Messenger. And the older I get,
the more they multiply. So it will continue, until the moment
I stop getting messages.

Then it'll be my turn to come and live with one of you.

READING WALLS

There was hardly a soul in the carriage, which I found disappointing. The way I felt was quite like the sense of regret people have when they say, 'There's nothing to watch on TV tonight.'

In every country the metro is like a stage and an auditorium all at once. I enjoy the rapid change of cast and the feeling that the same actor never performs twice – unless by accident, but if that happens, there's little chance of us noticing, because the play has such a large cast and the stage is so spacious that we're unlikely to spot a repeat entrance by the same character. Nobody has the starring role, and there's no director to impose their taste on them. It's the most democratic form of theatre in the world, because it's the spectator who decides whom to look at. It's never possible to listen to any conversation all the way through. The spectator is condemned to an open-ended show that never includes the whole story from the first capital letter to the final full stop. The punchlines are very rarely heard. 'The Russkies have bought up the whole of Karlovy Vary now, can you imagine?' 'But I'm being extremely careful,' a woman replies. Unfortunately, new actors come on stage, forcing us to be resigned to the fading-out of the dialogue. We could accept that it was the actual punchline. But what did it mean? How should we interpret it? A task for the journey to the next station, where a new act will begin.

When I'm on the metro I feel as if I'm in contact with literary material as demanding as any avant-garde fiction – the dramatist builds up my expectations, but doesn't satisfy them. Though usually the carriage is like a theatre of mime, not drama. The performers have mute roles, only offering me their body language. It's a show presenting the struggle to stay upright on a moving, unsteady stage. A show demonstrating how selected groups of muscles are engaged in not falling over, and messing up the role can be a great pleasure to watch. If the standing actor is a thing of beauty in their effort, the sitting actor is a thing of beauty in their lack of effort. What I'm seeing then is a very personal portrait. The actor in the sitting role seems to have lost the sense that they're still performing. They stop holding in their stomach. If it's a woman, she stops tensing her face muscles. If it's a man, he stops holding his head up so that fewer spectators will see the white tonsure of skin amid his hair. The actor sitting without a stage partner has only himself to rely on, and emanates helplessness. Helplessness accumulates in the rolls of flesh visible above the buttocks if he's sitting in a way that lets us observe him from the side. In this situation there's nothing he can do about those folds. It's a show of weakness of will, which in a spectator like me prompts affection. If on top of that the actor closes his eyes, however hard he may insist that he's isolating himself from the audience behind the barrier of his eyelids, the audience may feel quite differently about it. And then we've got him! Some of the spectators are just waiting for this sort of moment, as if counting on the fact that between Můstek and Malostranská one of the actors will start performing the show of releasing his soul, which there, before our very eyes, is going to rise above the metro tunnel. Closing your eyes in a public situation makes it very like an intimate situation. Changes occur in the face, and I think that as soon as they close their eyes every actor, even if they're playing a despicable character, becomes the epitome of sweetness and goodness.

But maybe that's just my projection, because I'd like to see them all with their eyes closed. I'm firmly convinced it gives us a sense of power. The person who's looking has power over the person who isn't looking. Or perhaps, behind his closed eyelids, the actor is waiting to see what the spectator's going to do to him? Maybe he's ready for anything? For a stranger to kiss him or slap him in the face?

2

So the cast was scanty: a couple of students, too far away for me to feel as if I were in a box at the theatre. I soon discovered that for the time being I was going to experience not theatre, but pure literature. I spotted a board on the carriage wall, the sort where they post advertisements. As I was learning Czech at the time, and enjoyed testing myself to see if I could understand a text or not, I started reading about how someone would soon come out of the shade of the chestnut trees:

> Soon I will come out of the shade of the chestnut trees
> and of bird song
> and will walk along the heated asphalt
> downhill around the bend
> from where I can see myself
> watching in the shade of the chestnut trees
> myself walking in a hat
> along the black asphalt
> from where I can see myself
> as I disappear
> around the bend, for ever
> out of sight*

I read the poem once, then again, and a third time, to make sure the same thing happened. At the words 'in a hat' I felt an alarming wobble in my intestines, as if my body were sending an electric current through them.

The poem was posted on the wall of the train as part of the 'Poems on the Underground' project, and it was signed 'Viola Fischerová'.

---

* All the quotations from Czech in this text were translated by Alex Zucker (unless otherwise stated).

The train reached Anděl station. I read the text several times more, until I probably knew it by heart, but I decided to write it down in my notebook. Suddenly, the director brought dozens of extras on stage, a woman jostled me, and the board featuring the poem was shielded by a policeman. *Stanice Smíchovské nádraží, vystupujte vlevo, ve směru jízdy.** The policeman got off. With my notebook on my knees, pleased to have jotted down almost all of the poem, I realized I was living a lie.

How easily we lie to avoid causing trouble. This motivation renders a lie innocent, of course, and in my eyes makes it a noble expedient.

To think of all the times I've lied to a poet!

A poet never gives you a poem to read – they shove it under your nose. And then shamelessly question you: 'Do you like it?' They never ask: 'Don't you like it?' And telling a poet 'Your poem leaves me cold' would be like spitting in their face.

But you have to say something. So I've come up with a wonderful lie.

'You know what,' I tell them, 'to feel a poem properly you have to tune its rhythm to your own rhythm, as Kapuściński once said. But I'm finding it harder and harder for my inner rhythm to harmonize with any poetry at all. It's as if I were doomed to some awful, vulgar rhythm from the outside, from the street, from TV... So I'd really better not desecrate your poem with my clumsy reading.'

---

* Czech: 'Next stop Smíchov Railway Station, exit on the left.'

'I understand you perfectly,' says the poet, because they too think that apart from their poems everything in the world is unbearable.

In fact, poets are usually quite happy to find that someone else is prepared to express their reservations about reality, just as they do.

This elegant lie allows me to endure encounters with poets, some of whom are insatiable and greedy. I'm afraid that as soon as I praise their poem, they'll grab me in their open jaws and tongue-press me into the next one. I'll be stuck there, crushed by someone else's talent.

But here, on Line B of the Prague Metro, all that proved to be untrue: no rhythm, no world, no metro, not even a police-man can present an obstacle when you come upon

THE RIGHT POEM.

I went home and – an act I regard as rather grandiose for a thirty-eight-year-old man – started sending the poem to my friends, in my own awkward translation.

Next day I went to the local library to look up 'Fischerová, Viola' (in 2004 I didn't have a smartphone, and even the flat I had rented for the week had no broadband; to dig around online I used internet cafés, but this time I decided to find the name in a proper library catalogue).

'Fischerová, Viola (1935), born in Brno, Czech poet and translator.'

3

She published her first collection of poetry at the age of fifty-seven.

With the title *Requiem for Pavel Buksa*.

She wrote it following her husband's suicide.

Her next collection appeared when she was fifty-eight, and the third on her sixtieth birthday. The Czechs discovered this mature poet, and a flood of prizes came in.

The librarian started looking for a magazine in which 'there was lots about Mrs Fischerová recently... But which paper was it? Just fancy – in her youth, both Hrabal and Havel were in love with her. Somewhere I read that one time they were walking along Spálená Street to the paper pulping plant – the place where Hrabal worked, do you know his book *Too Loud a Solitude*? – so they were walking along, Hrabal on one side, Havel on the other, and Fischerová in the middle. She was licking an ice cream. First she gave it to one of them to lick, then the other, by turns. Where is that magazine?'

4

Who hasn't read *Too Loud a Solitude*, about the man who recycles waste paper? He crushes old newspapers and books in a hydraulic press. But he provides salvation to a chosen few that he takes home with him. He saves the ones he thinks will tell him something he doesn't yet know about himself.

When he spots the spine of a valuable book, he calculates if he has the strength to open it. Whenever he decides that, yes, he has, he picks it up, and the book quivers in his fingers like a bride's wedding bouquet as she stands before the altar.

Unfortunately, although he never stops reading and looking for a sign in these books, he feels as if they're conspiring against him, and he never gets a single message from heaven.

5

'What about Hrabal's *Advertisement for a House I Don't Want to Live In*,* do you know it? He borrowed that title from one of Ms Fischerová's poems. But both men, I'll have you know, both Hrabal and Havel fell out of love with her when she met her first husband. He was a writer too. She emigrated to Switzerland with him, and then he killed himself there.'

I still have the photocopy of an interview which that librarian found for me fourteen years ago. The interviewer asks Viola Fischerová what prompted her to start writing after her husband's suicide.

'A year after my second husband, Josef Jedlička, and I had "found each other", we went on a trip to visit Pavel's grave in Basel. In the car on the way, I suddenly saw his face just the other side of the windscreen, but so close up that I had a

---

* This is the Czech title of a book published in English as *Mr. Kafka and Other Tales from the Time of the Cult*, translated by Paul Wilson, New Directions, 2015.

20

dreadful shock. Perhaps we're going to be killed, I thought, and Pavel has come to escort us to the next world. But nothing happened to us, and on the way back I jotted something down on a piece of paper. For the first time in decades. And next day something told me it was a key poem. It was "The Doorway to Our House", from my collection *Requiem for Pavel Buksa*. And it went on from there.'

> The doorway to our house
> the entrance to an open wound
> The stairway glistens
> Not a drop of blood
> Not a feather
> Our entire life
> lasted sixteen years
> and played out in three rooms

'At first,' Viola Fischerová goes on, 'I thought this was a way to discover the meaning of Pavel's death, and then the writing would come to a stop. But suddenly the poems started sprouting offshoots about other things entirely. That was how it started.'

6

From the library I went to the main post office to look her up in the phone book.

'Hello... No, I don't want anything... I'd just like to say that I read your poem on the metro... I'm not sure what else there is to add... No, I'm Polish. It's just that I read your poem, and it made such a strong impression on me that I felt I had to tell you.'

7

'Whatever surrounds us touches us in a recast of ideas, or speech – spoken, written or imaged speech.' This obvious fact (though for many who regard language as a mirror of reality it's not so obvious) was formulated by a poet.

'All the more so,' he continues, 'everything that has passed away is available to us only in the double recast to which the mind once subjected it, and to which it subjects it now. The past does not exist in any other form. Whoever would say otherwise simply states that the kaleidoscope of time, incomprehensible in each of its quarter-seconds, is present in some sort of super-mind, which beholds the past, the present and the future simultaneously.'*

I had underlined this quotation from Czesław Miłosz about the workings of the mind in relation to reality long ago. It was just waiting for its moment. It fits perfectly in this collection of texts about NOT THERE.

And so – all we ever get is the feeble report of memory.

---

* Czesław Miłosz, *Unattainable Earth*, translated by Czesław Miłosz and Robert Hass, Ecco Press, 1986.

My discovery of Viola Fischerová occurred in December 2004. I wrote the previous section of this story – recreating what I said over the phone – in early April 2018. I was almost one hundred per cent certain that this was how our conversation sounded to me as I stood in the phone booth at the post office.

In fact, I'd have sworn it.

But towards the end of April, while googling Viola, I found some notes from her diary of fourteen years ago that had been published on the internet, where she wrote:

'24 December 2004. This morning a man called who didn't introduce himself, but wanted to know my postal address. He said he had a nice surprise for me. He must be Father Christmas.

'1 January 2005. The man called again, and asked for my postal address again, because apparently he'd written it down wrong. I asked to whom I was speaking, if not Father Christmas. "It's going to be a surprise," said the mystery caller, and hung up.'

8

So memory's a fuck-up. Or: what the fuck, so much for memory!

That's what Viola and I would have said to each other over a glass of red wine. Or maybe not, maybe she wouldn't have taken it that seriously. She'd have said, oh well, so much for memory, *kurvanoga*...

It's hard to explain why she added the word *noga* ('leg') to the word *kurva* (literally 'whore', but a swearword on a par with 'fuck'). That was her special *przeklątko* ('swearwordlet'), as her good friend and translator of her poems into Polish, Dorota Dobrew, calls it – a word she used to drop into her less serious remarks. Because whenever she talked about things that really did prompt her to swear, she didn't soften the *kurva* by adding a *noga*.

So all right, Viola, *kurvanoga*, so much for memory! Witness accounts are often contradictory, because remembering things isn't a form of passive registration – our memory doesn't record everything democratically, but makes an active recording, fitting the facts to our assumptions. We alter the past to make our memories fit the whole of the remembered image.

(This idea belongs in a lecture on neurology, rather than a reporter's impression-ology.)

9

In my first email to Viola I wrote that I had been sending her poem about coming out of the shade of the chestnut trees to various friends in Poland and the Czech Republic as a Christmas and New Year present. Our sense of pleasure, as mankind realized long ago, is limited unless we share it with someone else.

Some of my Polish friends were surprised to find that the Czechs have a metaphysical poet. (They do, a poet from the metro. After all, the less of God you have, the greater your need for the metaphysical!)

They had reacted very warmly. 'What a fine poem,' they wrote, because they're intelligent, they know they should use short, plain words. 'Dead', not 'he who has passed away', or 'at the end of the road'. (I learned that from Julian Barnes, and I think he learned it from Gustave Flaubert.)

Viola (in her diary) was pleased when on 24 January a 'two-metre email' arrived listing the reactions of Polish readers to her poem. She quoted in its entirety a letter from 'a man with whom Mariusz has corresponded for quite a time, without knowing his identity'. (That's how she described him, and now I 'remember' that he may have been a young teacher from Silesia, but what was his name?)

'Viola Fischerová's poem', he wrote, 'is ideal for public transport. Its structure and content present the situation of someone who's on a journey – after, during and before; the subject is both a separate object as well as a part of the whole – it's like looking at your own reflection in the window of a rapidly moving train carriage while travelling in a defined direction, within a constantly changing landscape.

'And as for this: "...from where I can see myself / as I disappear / around the bend, for ever / out of sight". Sometimes when I look at people, it's as if I were looking at myself, and when I listen to them, it's as if I'm listening to myself. Like in Wim Wenders' *Wings of Desire*, in which, as he passes people, the character we might call the Angel hears their thoughts, and sometimes escorts them, inside them, to the brink, beyond which this observed "self" disappears from sight and ceases to be audible. THIS IS PURE GENIUS.

'I'm reminded of a scene from another film, in which a man is wandering about in a castle. Suddenly, he finds himself in a hall that he can't leave, however hard he tries, because he keeps encountering a woman who comes running out of the wall, falls by the stairs and is stabbed with a sword by another "ghost" who runs after her. This sequence recurs every time the man tries to leave the hall and go into the passage. Each time, we see the extraordinary visions that the main character is seeing. I can't remember how the scene ends. I have a similar feeling of being caught in a time loop now, as if I've fallen into a miraculous stream of consciousness. AS YOU CAN SEE, THE POEM HAS HAD AN EFFECT ON ME. P.S. Reading something like that on the metro must be an astonishing experience.'

So said the reader, a precious one – as it turned out – for Viola too.

10

Dear Viola, there's something I've only just realized.

Thanks to you – or rather, thanks to the fact that from our very first phone conversation our relationship was quite un-usual – I've had an idea: I'm going to write 'I remember'.

In the first person singular, this particular verb should always be put in quotation marks. That would be the most honest way to treat one's readers.

'I remember' that the first time we clapped eyes on each other, in the spring, you came and stood outside your block in Prague's Barrandov housing estate so that I wouldn't get lost on my way from the Chaplin Square metro station.

'I remember' that as we were waiting for the lift, you said: 'This block is home to lots of re-emigrants, who escaped Czechoslovakia after 1968, and then came back in the early 1990s. In this country, the people who have returned are not respected. They say we betrayed them, we left them in the communist shit. And we also remind them that they failed to emigrate. Are people who've returned respected in Poland?'

'I remember' answering: 'Very much. They impress us.'

'I remember' that once we were sitting at the table and you said: 'They don't respect Havel either, because his existence reminds them that they weren't heroes. They do everything they can to strip him of heroism, to diminish his bravery, just to make sure no one can see what cowards they were.'

'I remember' that your eyes were blue, and time hadn't taken away their colour. You had chestnut hair, almost black in fact, with no signs of grey. It was long, but you tied it in a bun.

'I remember' being in the lift and thinking: How amazing that, amid the great mixture of humanity on the metro, amid all the garish signs on the carriage walls, amid all the chaos of the city, it's so easy for one particular individual to stand out!

'I remember' you looking for your lighter, then blowing out smoke as you explained that everything immediately becomes the past. The present doesn't exist.

'I remember' saying that my dad can't bear looking at the second hand on his watch because it moves at a speed that terrifies him.

'I remember' you saying that we're not capable of halting the here and now. How long does it last? A few seconds?

So there was Hrabal on one side, Havel on the other, and Viola in the middle with her ice cream.

'Sorry to disappoint, but I must put you straight,' she declared during our first evening together. 'Havel was on one side of me, but the man on the other side was Honza Zábrana, a poet in those days. We were on our way to see Hrabal. We were going to the waste-paper recycling centre, where he crushed books in his hydraulic press. We found him in the mildewed courtyard in the act of stamping paper flat.'

Honza, officially Jan Zábrana, later well known as a trans-lator of Russian and American prose and poetry, confirms it in his diary; it was August 1958, Viola was carrying a cone of pistachio-flavoured ice cream, and had already stained her top – a snow-white one, as ever – which she kept handing to them left and right to have a lick, and he was taking Hrabal the first Czech edition of Isaac Babel's stories.

Bohumil Hrabal opens his 1965 short-story collection *Advertisement for a House I Don't Want to Live In* with one of her poems: 'The dairy could even sell at night. / To start an independent life is more than to be born. / Disbelief can be understood / as indiscriminate attention. / Anyway I'm placing an advertisement for a house / I don't want to live in.' When they saw the name Viola Fischerová underneath the poem, many readers thought she was a made-up person because they'd never heard of her before.

When I tried to compile her biography for myself, I soon found out that she was destined to the life of an artist as soon as she was born. And there's no better way to put it, because:

In 1935, her father, Josef Ludvík Fischer, a philosopher ('philosophy is bound to be metaphysical'), asked the poet František Halas ('the major poet of a chaotic era') to think up a name for his daughter. They both thought Květa (meaning 'flower') was too banal, and Růžena (meaning 'rose') too funereal.

As well as choosing her name, Halas wrote a poem to celebrate her birth ('Maybe one day this little girl will dream, / the decaying poet will turn in his grave, / the child's eyes will carry me to heaven... / And this moment is mine to await – František Halas wishes Violka everything she doesn't have.'

When, as teenagers, she and her schoolfriends went to see the great poet Vladimír Holan ('Holan, librarian of God'), he read her first poem and said: 'I'm sorry to say it's as transparent as spring water.' Six months later, when she showed him the next one, he said: 'Yes, it's getting more opaque...'

When, at the age of twenty, she dropped the poet Honza Zábrana, he wrote a poem about her that began with the words: 'I haven't sent you anywhere, / there are plenty of women in hell...' She dedicated one of hers to him, which began: 'He frightened her like live meat under a tenderizer. / But still she grasped after happiness...'

For her, poets were saints and poetry a religion. She often said that she was very demanding of her own texts, because they had to be sacred items. 'And that was the source of my out-and-out ruinous self-criticism.'

And so, at the age of twenty-four, she stopped writing. 'Occasionally,' she told me, 'I'd write something when I was drunk and put it in the bedside cabinet, but next morning I'd throw it away without reading it.'

The main cause of her silence was the poetry written by a close friend of hers from the same crowd that included Havel and Zábrana, later known as the '36 generation. Havel said that in the gloomy 1950s they tried to give positive meaning to their childish desires. They were between fifteen and twenty years old, and their vitality was stronger than Stalinism. The friend was called Věra Linhartová, and most of the time she said nothing. Viola regarded her poetry as perfection, against which she simply couldn't compete. 'I knew,' she recalled, 'what Věra had made out of what, and what it meant within the text, and that destroyed me. Sometimes in her presence I felt like a mouse before a snake. That's why I kept quiet for thirty years.'

She took a degree in Slavic studies at Charles University, which she had begun at Brno University, then she worked as an editor for Czechoslovak Radio. In 1968 she and her future husband Pavel Buksa (whose pen name was Karel Michal) emigrated to Basel, in Switzerland, where she studied German and history. She worked as a teacher at nursing and technical schools. In 1984 she moved to Germany to work for Radio Free

Europe. There she married her second husband, essayist and novelist Josef Jedlička, who for most of his life was banned from publication in Czechoslovakia. In 1994, after being widowed again, she returned to Prague.

1 2

An email dated 17 March 2009:

'Mariusz, I forgot to add that in the 1950s, when I stopped writing, Hrabal said: "Linhartová has burned your brains out." Thirty years later, in Prague, when I brought a copy of my first collection to the pub for him, he read it, and a week later he said: "Pavel's death was more powerful than the spell Linhartová put on you. That's beautiful."

'Then he looked at me across the table, scowled and said: "But that won't save you."'

1 3

Viola met Pavel Buksa through a dead cat.

An indefinite dark mass had thumped softly against the window-pane, knocked the unlatched half of the window open and landed with a plop on the settee... The body of a cat lay oddly twisted on the green repp fabric, its black coat shining in the light of the desk lamp like warm, soft asphalt... It couldn't have been dead long, because the body wasn't yet in rigor, and its wide-open yellow eyes in their slanting slits were as bright as in a live animal... The reporter did not like cats. Alive or dead. Anyone not enamoured of live cats is surely least likely to pay them much respect when dead.

'Who chucked you in here, beast?' he asked impiously.

'You don't know,' the cat said, 'he didn't tell you his name.'

Its position meanwhile remained unchanged and its mouth barely moved to the sound of the words. Its voice was faint. A little hoarse, but not quite how we would imagine a cat's voice...

'Say "sixteen",' the reporter challenged the cat.

'Sixteen,' said the cat.

'Eighteen and a half.'

'Eighteen and a half.'

'Accumulation of capital.'

'Accumulation of capital,' said the cat, without batting an eyelid.

The reporter didn't know what should come next. He wasn't sure of having read it anywhere.

'Do you want some nice milk?' he asked, for the sake of saying something...

'You don't want anything,' said the cat. 'You is dead. Being dead, you doesn't eat.'...

'How long have you been dead?'

'A very long time. You doesn't know exactly, you can't remember. You isn't good at guessing time.'...

'And why do you talk?'

'Because you's been asked questions.'*

---

* From 'The Dead Cat' by Karel Michal, translated by David Short, in *Everyday Spooks*, Karolinum Press, 2008. The italicized text quoted here is from that edition.

A doctor examined the animal, and found that even though its heart had stopped beating, none of its internal organs were working and it was as hard as rock, it was very knowledgeable. It knew lots of languages, and replied to every question in the language in which it was asked. It only had one shortcoming: it didn't know how to conjugate verbs in the first person singular. It always replied in the second person. All the cat's remarks – as a Czech would say – were deadly logical.

For example, to the question 'What is a worker?' the cat replied: 'A worker is a man who gains his livelihood through manual labour, and who lacks the requirements for earning it dishonestly.'

Because the cat said exactly what it thought, which meant that it might cause trouble, it ended up in a closed monastic community.

Working as an editor for radio, Viola decided to broadcast a dramatized version of 'The Dead Cat'. It included some passages that were rather iconoclastic for those days, and instead of abridging them herself, she decided to seek the author's help. So she went to the Prague suburb of Zbraslav, where thirty-six-year-old Pavel Buksa lived on the market square among his beloved antiques, which he bought from dealers. 'And there I stayed,' she said.

'Miss Fischerová, are you seeing anyone?' asked Pavel the next day.

'What of it?'

'I'd like to keep you for myself...'

'And then, after seven months together and three weeks of Soviet occupation we ran away to Switzerland.'

'The Dead Cat' is from Karel Michal's cult short-story collection *Everyday Spooks*. As in *The Master and Margarita*, the rational world is invaded by the irrational. For example, Houska, who paves the streets, accidentally hatches an egg. According to folklore, a chicken hatched by a person is bound to increase its master's riches by helping with his work. The chicken cobbles the streets with great tenacity. An accountant finds he's capable of changing into a bear and decides to use this advantage to get himself a more interesting job. But the people at the circus tell him there's nothing special about changing into a bear, nor will a bear accountant impress anyone either, because there are dozens of animals that can count.

In the early 1960s, the significance of Karel Michal's stories was understood in a flash. The readers sucked up all the associations just as a hungry dog licks the marrow out of a bone. They stripped it bare of hidden meanings. (As for the lifeless cat, in a totalitarian system even the dead are dangerous and must be silenced.) Between 1961 and 1967 *Everyday Spooks* was reprinted four times, meaning a total of 100,000 copies, which in a small country like Czechoslovakia was a gigantic print run. What can we learn from it today? The same as from *The Good Soldier Švejk*, a novel that, in its time, was nothing but 'a vulgar collection of anecdotes', but which changed into a philosophical work without a single line of text being altered.

'Mariusz,' Viola wrote, '*Spooks* is a work of humour, but at a deeper level it's about being disappointed by people.' And she asked me to do something to promote its first Polish edition, published in 2008.

The writer Ivan Klíma noted that in *Spooks* a voice was given to the author's – i.e. Karel Michal's – phantoms, which never left the man – i.e. Pavel Buksa.

14

How careful we must be about making definite statements. I learned to put 'dead', rather than 'passed away', and that is the school I profess. But when I started looking for information about Viola's husband in my favourite biographical dictionary of twentieth-century Czech writers, I found a comment about Pavel Buksa / Karel Michal that I thought beautiful, and abandoned my former principles.

This is what Radko Šťastný, the author of the dictionary, wrote about him: 'Dobrovolně odešel ze života', which literally means 'He voluntarily left this life'. But in the entries for other writers who committed suicide, he put 'Zemřel sebevraždou': 'He died as the result of suicide.'

The indirect forms of expression sometimes still used in Czech literary writing, such as *poprvé spatřila světlo světa* – literally, 'she/it first saw the light of day' – instead of 'was born' (of a girl) or 'was published' (of a book), make me feel the same way as I do about antique cutlery. I can try to eat with those knives and forks at festive occasions, but I'm reluctant to use them on an everyday basis, because they're large and unwieldy, and they look pretentious when all you're having is pork chops. Nevertheless, those old-fashioned words about voluntarily leaving this life seem to me full of dignity and respect.

As a phrase to describe death, it's highly aesthetic.

I wonder if Radko Šťastný wrote it about Pavel Buksa / Karel Michal consciously or accidentally? If it was deliberate, I see it as an attempt to understand the act, as if the eminent historian of literature were accepting the writer's way of ending his own life.

'For me, it's like a memorial of understanding in miniature. A very rare thing,' I wrote in a letter to Viola.

The result was the longest conversation we ever had. ('Come over, I'll have to get drunk to tell you how my poems came to be written.') During that evening she marked each memory with the relevant label: 1) 'This you can write about while I'm still alive'; 2) 'This you can only write about after my death'; 3) 'This you can never write about, not even after my death.'

I'm sticking to these rules.

The time has come for point 2.

15

'He wrote that Pavel voluntarily left this life?'

She looks for her lighter.

She hands me the corkscrew.

'All of a sudden, I had a wonderful dream that I was walking along a bridge... This was on 30 June 1984, in Basel. I knew that dream from childhood, because it had often recurred. One time it would be brown and white, another time in full colour. There was always a lady coming towards me in a dressing gown with the hood up, smiling at me very nicely. Suddenly, her smile would tense, deaden and turn to stone. I would start to feel afraid of her, and I'd fly away from there in terror. I'd fall from the bridge head first, into the river, and if I flew further, it was onto grass. As a child I had that dream about thirty times. The last time I'd had it was at the age of twenty-two. But now in the dream, in Basel, when I was almost fifty, I needed a dressing gown too. Just like that lady's. So, still in the dream, I bought one at a department store, a pink one. But I realized Pavel wouldn't like it, so I went back and returned it. I remember saying: "My husband will object to it." The sales assistants were annoyed by my respect for my husband... Then I walked on, and I saw another lovely dressing gown in a shop window. A white one, which I immediately bought, and I knew Pavel would like it. The day after this dream, I really was walking down the street, and suddenly I did see an exquisite snow-white towelling dressing gown in a shop window. The one from my dream! So I bought it instantly, thinking Pavel was sure to like it. I also bought a pair of sandals. We had identical taste, so in normal circumstances he'd have seen the things I'd bought and he'd have said: "Great." But all of a sudden I felt afraid of showing them to him at all. And I had a feeling something was up, because when I got home, the first thing he said was: "I saw a lovely man's dressing gown that would suit you better." "But look how pretty and elegant this one is," I said. "It's pretty, but it's bourgeois," he said, "and I've chosen you a lovely, unpretentious one instead." "Well," I said, "I can have two dressing gowns, can't I?" I should add that at the time he'd just come back from rehab. I poured him a beer – I was furtively giving him non-alcoholic beer, which I used to pour into empty bottles of the real kind at night. That evening I had to take some strong pills, because not long before I'd cut myself while opening a beer for him. In just two days, the small spot on my hand had changed into a painful stripe. I could see that it was still advancing, and I was afraid it was blood poisoning, so I went to the doctor. It turned out that my own organism had eaten away half my thyroid gland. Suddenly, I started having trouble with my skin too, which felt incredibly itchy. "Your immune system is down," said the doctor. I started taking some new medicine. And on the day I bought the dressing gown, I thought I had everything ready for school. At the time, I was teaching legal know-how at a technical school. I was no expert on law, and had only just learned German, but I prepared each lesson very well. I thought that, as I already had the material for my pupils ready, I could take the tablets. They made me feel very dopey. They had such a strong tranquillizing effect that after taking them I could only mindlessly watch television, or doze. Just then a friend of ours knocked at the door, a wonderful fellow, who had a wife, although he was gay. She was extremely intelligent and loved him very much, but why on earth were they together? He had lots of boyfriends, but I think she must have been a masochist, oh well... Pavel said: "Viola, there's something I have to explain to Thomas, but I can't do it sober. Two beers! Just two beers..." So I gave them to him. I don't know what they talked about. I think Thomas was in love with an Arab, and Pavel was his confidant. At ten o'clock Thomas went home, and I had a snooze in front of the television. First Ukšuk, our dog, put his head on one of my knees, then Pavel laid his head on the other one and said: "I had the most dreadful dream... I was a policeman, and a girl came up to me, shouting that she could hear footsteps! And they were getting closer. She asked me to save her. So I said: 'I'm just an ordinary policeman.' And she said: 'But my life is at stake.' And I had this terrible sense of impotence because I couldn't help her..." He said it all into my stomach, with his head on my knee. So I said: "Pavel, a drunken mind has drunken dreams. Let's go to bed." I went to brush my teeth, and next time I looked he was sitting in the kitchen. "Come to bed," I said. "Wait a moment, darling," he said, "wait a moment, just two more beers, just two." I fetched him those two bottles. It was like with my second husband, Jedlička, who wasn't meant to smoke, so to stop him from smoking too much I started finishing off his cigarettes, and that was how I got hooked. I'll drink some of the beer for him, I thought. And that's how a scene that was straight out of Ionesco got started. How come I never thought of putting it that way before? It was pure Ionesco: I wanted to buy you that dressing gown, but you didn't want it... No, it's not that I didn't want it, I'd already bought myself another one. Yes, but I wanted to buy you the men's one... All right, I bought myself a dressing gown... and so it went, on and on, in various forms. I was under the influence of the pills, and I'd had some beer, so by now I felt as if I were in another world. I was so sleepy I was falling off my chair. I said: "Listen, I'm off to bed. And I've had enough of all this." So my final remark was negative. I went to bed. You have to know that Pavel's entire family was obsessed with guns. His father shot himself towards the end of the war. His mother always had a small Derringer, a lady's pistol. On the rare occasions when Pavel and I argued, it was about that, because he had a fixation too. He was always trying to force me to have a gun. I'd say: "Go to hell! If I have a gun, I'll be disturbed by unwanted thoughts about who to fire it at, sod off with your gun!" One night in Basel, I was walking down a dark street on my way to visit a friend when a man attacked me, but that was no reason for me to carry a gun. I wanted to buy you that dressing gown, but you didn't want it... I fell asleep. Pavel, who was always quoting the nice maxim "Never let the sun go down on your anger!" woke me up at once and said: "Don't worry, you can have two dressing gowns, it's not a problem." To which I said: "Pavel, let me get to sleep now." And then he said: "The man's one would suit you better, I'd like to buy it for you..." And he kept waking me up every few minutes. He was usually so tactful, but there must have been something wrong; the pills had dulled my brain and I didn't react. There was never any question of breaking up. Never. Just once, there was a phase when I would go to a girlfriend's place to study. When he was drunk, he had to talk to me. But once we were living abroad I was often busy. I had to do a lot of preparing, read a lot of those idiotic legal texts.... I didn't know the language very well, and I wasn't familiar with the Swiss legal system, but by some miracle I had managed to become a teacher. Of law! I couldn't lose the job, especially as I'd worked as a cloakroom attendant in an English pub at first. What's more, Pavel was a nightwatchman. A talented, highly acclaimed author, a scriptwriter whose film *Honour and Glory*, based on his own book, had won first prize in Venice – working as a watchman. So I went to a girlfriend's place to study, because she had three rented rooms and peace and quiet. And I managed to learn something completely impossible, as I like to say. At the time, he said: "All right, you go off to her place." And I think that was the only time when I distanced myself from him a little. But now those conversations while I was trying to sleep... I wanted to buy you such a lovely dressing gown... So finally I said: "Leave me alone, I've had enough." At which Pavel got up and went over to his own bed; he had an American revolver, and he said: "This will solve everything." Suddenly I heard a loud "Bang!" Once, when he was drunk, he'd fired at the kitchen door, and this time I thought he'd shot at the ceiling. I looked up, and he was lying there, under a quilt. I raised it and saw that he wasn't moving, and below his heart there was a scorch mark.'

Viola moves her glass, and from under the newspapers on the table she pulls out a volume of poetry.

In the end what counts is a bullet
In the end what counts is an unspoken word
In the end nothing adds up

But the fly
I didn't kill the day before yesterday
is still here flying around

'I called the ambulance and my girlfriend. They arrived quickly, Pavel was still alive, and the doctor asked him: "Mr Buksa, were you feeling unhappy?"'

16

We are familiar with the sorrow of horses, the sorrow of dogs, not prompted by any external cause. I believe that even an earthworm knows sorrow, in keeping with the capacity for judgement it needs in order to survive. We humans attempt to give it a name, but it does not disappear. It is indestructible, and cannot be tamed. There is no need to speak of it every day of the week, but we can get used to it when we listen to what sorrow says.

I, sorrow, am with you. I alone am your sorrow, for other people's sorrows are embarrassed in your presence; they hide away, trying not to lose face. I share your bed, your bread and salt; without me, you would not even know their taste. I rock you to sleep in my arms, I cover you as you sleep, and you wake when you think of me. I clothe you and feed you, for it is through me and me alone that you are stubborn or submissive, foolish or wise, that in the eyes of others you are valuable or worthless. I, sorrow, lead you into every drama, to what you did or did not want to be, and what you are, however badly you did not want to know. I am even to blame for the sort of lies you tell others and which you confess to yourself, I am also to blame for the fact that you do not feel that you are to blame. I lead you to seek and to not find, and to be what it is that seeks. I know how to pretend, how to be little and hide in the corner, how to be big, and how to hide you away. I am all of your loves, never your hatred, which is why you do not feel it even where you should. Yet now that you have recognized me, you will always see my reflection flickering in the water, whether it is fast-flowing or old and stagnant. And should you want a soul, you have one, because I, sorrow, am your soul in its entirety, your sympathy and lack of it, your deeds both good and evil, and your awareness of what they are. Together, the two of us call that life. We have grown used to each other. We are nothing but each other, and that is what we call life. Once you know me well enough, I will lead you to death like a docile lamb, stripped of its wool, and I will no longer be with you after that, for I, sorrow, have nothing but you...

Karel Michal, 'Charming Neighbours', 1972

17

'To be an exile, I think you have to have an innate talent for it. Pavel was very introverted, and if he did ever communicate anything, he did it through a joke. Just before he shot himself he'd spent two months in a psychiatric hospital, where he went through rehab. Professor Ladewig said that his basic problem wasn't alcoholism, but a loss of identity. "That's the diagnosis, Mrs Buksová. He has a brick wall in front of him and he's not able to form a relationship with his environment. He's emotionally walled in. Please note that he can't write about himself in either the first or the third person." When the movie he co-wrote won the top foreign film prize at the 1969 Venice Film Festival, where Fellini's *Satyricon* won the award for the best Italian movie, our friends said: "Apply to Swiss television, you're holding a trump card now." At the time, he was working as a watchman, doing the rounds of some warehouses at night on a bicycle to make sure everything was in order. And Pavel replied: "I didn't come to Switzerland to play the great script-writer who won a major award." Some time later he managed to get a job at a classical high school, where he taught Latin and Greek. But he couldn't write. He said he didn't have his public here. And that he needed time. But the more time went by, the more firmly he locked himself away. In 1972 we were both asked to write texts for a collection called *Czechs in Switzerland: A Cold Paradise*. And Pavel's voice in "Charming Neighbours" prompted lots of reaction. But he never wrote anything else in those fifteen years.

'Here's "Charming Neighbours" for you, keep it.'

'Going back to that night... I was starting to have an excruciating headache, but I had to go to the police station. There I sat, the officer questioned me, and I told him about the dressing gowns. The policeman was called Holzman, and he really was a man of wood. I asked him: "Have you any headache pills? This is intolerable." He just kept smiling and saying: "No, we haven't got any." During the questioning an older man came in a few times. He'd listen for a while and then leave the room again. Suddenly, this man asked: "When did you see the gun?" "When I raised the quilt it was lying there, so I put it aside." You have to know I had traces of gunpowder on my left hand. Then the fellow named Holzman took me home. I asked if he believed in God. He said he did. I told him: "I'm feeling the most awful fear, I once read in a book that suicides end up in impenetrable darkness. In a void where there's nothing at all." It horrified me, I was worried about him. Ladewig, the psychiatrist, once told me: "Basically, Pavel is your child."

'I don't know how to talk about poetry. The only comment I ever make is that a person can even use poetry to defend himself. Listen:

> I cannot reach you
> You are not here
> Neither dead
> Nor alive

And by the kitchen window
in a chair
a void sits slump-shouldered
drinking and staring blankly

'It went on for four years – until 1988! The whole time I felt
terrified about what was happening to Pavel there. Until Josef
and I came upon a modest little church – compared with a
baroque or Gothic one it was nothing at all. But there were two
priests there, an older one, who had a bullet from the Battle of
Stalingrad in his head, and a young one who interpreted the
Old and New Testaments in an extremely intelligent way; later
on I was baptized by him. Josef was a highly educated Catholic,
and after lunch on Sundays, once we'd had our coffee, we'd take
Ukšuk for a walk and talk non-stop about the young priest's ser-
mons. Josef saved me a lot of money on psychotherapy, because
I was always telling him about the dark void. One time I said:
"Pavel isn't in the least to blame for shooting himself, because
he was dragged into a vortex of illness that he couldn't get out
of." And I burst into tears. Josef leaned over me, took me by the
wrists, like this, and said: "Viola, it was for people like him that
Jesus died." And from that moment on my fear was gone. It was
as if someone had flushed it out of me.

'But there was one thing I couldn't flush away.

'Would you hand me my lighter?

'After the police interview I got into a sort of vicious circle.
I'd be walking along with Ukšuk, and I'd start thinking: "If they

decide that I killed Pavel, I'll get so many years in jail that I'll never see this dear little dog again. Thomas will have to take a picture of him so I can always have him with me." Then I'd think about the fact that my spine hurt all the time and I must keep going to the swimming pool. Would they let me swim in there? What would I do if my painkillers didn't work? The minute an absurd idea crept into my head the next one followed after it. And soon you're knee-deep in absurdities, even if you know they're quite irrelevant. But you can't get away from them. You create a sort of drama about yourself that bears no relation to reality. You know what, as soon as they told me Pavel was dead, I felt terribly cold – not on the surface, but somewhere deep inside. I got into the bath and ran the hot water but I still felt cold, it wouldn't stop, it went on and on. Suddenly, I looked up and saw that my foot was all red, but I still felt cold. "The water's poisoned," I thought to myself, and turned off the tap. And what do you know, my foot was scalded for the next two months. But at the time I couldn't feel a thing, nothing at all, just the cold. Because that coldness was inside me. And this poem is about that:

> Even he
> who does not kill a fly in spring
> can be suspected

> Even he
> who carries a giant child on his back
> can be suspected

47

Even he
whose soul
death scalds with cold
can be suspected

As I discovered yesterday

'That older man, the police commissioner, asked: "Do you know how it happened?" To which I said: "Please listen, Commissioner, I've seen enough crime movies to know that if I had wanted to kill Pavel, I'd bloody well have put on rubber gloves to make sure I didn't have traces of gunpowder on me." And he said... he said: "Mrs Buksová, not all cases are like in crime movies. We are guided by our experience and it will lead us to our goal." That was all, and then he amiably said goodbye. I managed to add: "Do you really think I killed him?" He didn't answer that question, he just said: "You've got a hard time ahead of you; if you need help or advice, here's my number." And he was gone. When I looked, the gun was still... still lying in the bedroom. I phoned him, what... what was I to do with it? He gave me an address I was to take it to. And I... I... never found anything as disgusting in all my life as... as... guns. Not frogs, not snakes, but guns – extremely disgusting. Once, I pulled a large frog out of a hedgehog's mouth because it couldn't swallow it, it was too big, and both creatures had had enough. I wasn't disgusted. But as for touching a gun! Would you like some more to drink?'

'Yes, there's the second bottle I brought.'

'I never like to have a second bottle in the house. So, the next day, they asked me to bring that gun to the prosecutor's office. There was another older man there, extremely sympathetic, who started talking to me, but as I was convinced they'd... they'd lock me up, I started telling that nice man about Ukšuk, that... that I had to have a large photo of him, would he please take one for me, because seven years from now I wouldn't see him again. And he said: "Mrs Buksová, for that you'd get life, not seven years." Imagine me at that moment. But he immediately added: "We've done our research, and we can see that your husband's body was not under stress when the bullet entered it. Your husband wasn't frightened, his muscles were relaxed." I understood this to mean his body hadn't defended itself. My first thought was that you could kill a person while they were asleep. I still refused to let go. "The trajectory definitely indicates suicide, Mrs Buksová, we are in no doubt." Now I'll... I'll tell you... something... something that I don't want published in my lifetime. Whenever I'm watching a play and I see that... that someone's suspected of something, I can't stand it, not for a single second. I'm quite incapable of watching a movie if the figure of a suspect appears. The very sound of that word instantly makes me feel that... that.... cold inside me again. Nobody could ever guess why I always leave the cinema at once.'

'My father...' she says, dragging on her cigarette. 'Did I tell you he was a philosopher? Before the war, before Buddhism was fashionable, he used to repeat the theory that everything is connected with everything else. And everything can act on everything else, meaning that everything forms an inter-woven unity.'

JERZY SZCZYGIEŁ
IN PRAGUE

'I've got to see that glorious city one last time, the place where you've worked so hard, son.'

He saw it one last time in 2009, then in 2010, and also in 2012. So this is his fourth one last time.

'Dad,' I ask on 7 June 2015, looking up from my laptop, 'I'm writing a piece about you in Prague – what should it say?'

'Well, my full name has to be there – Szczygieł, Jerzy. And it has to be light-hearted, not a heavy text,' he says, 'because in Prague everything's light-hearted. And,' he adds, 'make it interesting and delightful.'

'Yes,' Mama suddenly agrees, though she never says much, 'it should be delightful – otherwise, why write it?'

Hmm, no one has ever set me terms like those before.

Dad's needs are easily satisfied, he just has to switch on the Czech television set in the hotel room and he won't move all evening. He's thrilled by the channel where they play *dechovka*, an appalling racket played on wind instruments – the most primitive Bregović from the Kusturica movies is the high priest of subtlety by comparison. Thirty seconds of *dechovka* and I'm ready to throw up my own oesophagus.

'Ooooh!'

'Whaaat?'

'It's taking years off me,' says Dad from behind the telly.

A stream of *dechovka* hits pours out, by minor and major bands, one sixty-plus-year-old chanteuse after another. 'You know what,' says Dad, 'now I know why so many of the old girls in this country sing. It's because they don't go to church on Sundays like our lot, they just get up and sing a jolly tune instead. Our fanatical old biddies don't have that joy in them – the church kills it.'

At this point my mind comes to a halt and doesn't know which way to go, because Dad, who in Poland listens to the ultra-Catholic Radio Maria, has plainly been corrupted here in Prague.

He's sorry he can't speak Czech, though occasionally he rattles off three words. When he's in a good mood, he stands to attention and says: '*Vstupenka! Jizdenka! Letenka!* Tell me again: *vstupenka* is a ticket for a show, *jizdenka* is a ticket for a ride on the bus or tram, and *letenka* is for the aeroplane, right?' He can't get over the fact that a ticket can have three different names. I explain that the Czechs are at a higher level of civilization than many other nations, they've developed their language to have a single word where others have as many as three, for instance 'an', 'aeroplane', 'ticket'. 'So how did it go? Your friend from Poland wanted to go to a club with naked ladies and asked at the door for a *ticket for a ride*?'

Dad is unbelievably chatty, so he forces me to accost strangers for him. 'Don't forget, just Czechs – no one else is as interesting.' So at lunch in a restaurant garden I accost a plump man with brown hair and ginger stubble. His name is Jan, he's the manager of a hotel. 'Ask him,' says Dad (Jesus, in my old age I'm going to be just like him or worse, I can see it in myself already!), 'ask him what the Czechs are like.' So I'm supposed to just up and ask him what the Czechs are like, when I don't know him from Adam? 'Yes, because I want to know, after all, it's the fourth time I've been to Prague, and I still haven't asked.' So I ask the question, and this Jan fellow, aged 34, says the Czechs are dreadful and he doesn't like them. In fact, he doesn't like people in general. He only likes a person when he gets to know them better. And we can get to know each other too, but let's drink wine – it's such a corny Czech cliché to suggest beer, he adds. 'You gentlemen smell amazing,' says Jan. 'To smell aftershave on a Czech man is a miracle, and I'm sensitive to miracles thanks to having a job in a slightly better world.' 'Tell him,' says Dad, 'that my son buys me aftershave twice a year, and get him to tell us something about the Czechs.' 'He says the Czechs are gloomy,' I tell my dad. 'Indifferent to the world and introverted.' 'Not at all!' protests Dad, 'they're very jolly, for instance I bought this hat the second time we were in Prague, from the Vietnamese on Na Veselí Street, which means "Jolly" Street – where in Poland is there a street with a name like that? In our country there's nothing but gloom and Rydzyk.* What's more, when we came on holiday and stayed at Mr Milan's house, it was between Na Veselí Street and Na Lepším – "Better" Street. You can't do better than jolly and better.'

'Dad,' I say, 'Jan says the Czechs are very jolly, but only when they become close friends. They're jolly to each other, but they don't need the surrounding world at all – it could be stolen away and they wouldn't care.' 'That's why I like this nation,' says Dad, 'they never go abroad, they're self-sufficient, not like the Poles. Patriotism means not going away, unless it's to Prague for a couple of weeks, like me and my wifey.'

'You can even go for three,' adds Dad, when I read this text out to him.

'I'm telling you,' says Jan, whom my father has chosen to explain to him what the Czechs are like, 'on the whole people are all the same. I know that from my position at work – I've been at my job for fourteen years. These days I'm more than just a receptionist, of course. A Jew comes to our hotel and it's nothing but "Give me, give me, give me." An Arab comes and it's the same: "Give me, give me, give me." You people, I think to myself, why do you fight each other, when you're both exactly the same? Isn't it the truth that in the first instance neither of

---

* This is your translator speaking: I generally avoid adding footnotes to literary texts, but in this case the author has given me permission to explain a few things. Tadeusz Rydzyk is the controversial priest who founded the right-wing Catholic Radio Maria, a man who expresses inflammatory views.

you is able to stand himself? And as soon as you see yourself in the other guy, you want to commit hara-kiri on the spot, but as you haven't the courage to kill yourselves and you've still got to shag your wives at night, you commit hara-kiri, but on foreigners?"'

'No, that's not nice about shagging their wives, I don't want to hear such things,' says Dad. 'We're just about to eat, don't let that man ruin our lunch. Tell him the Czech language is very interesting.' 'To be frank with you,' says Jan, 'I don't like the sound of Polish, your language is terribly soft, like a child lisping, but our *čeština* is the harshest of the Slavic languages, it sounds almost as harsh as German.'

'Dad, let's be on our way or we won't be back in time to take Mama to the theatre. Is there one last thing you want to say to Jan?' 'What can I say off the cuff?' wonders my father. 'When two scythes have passed you by, you lose your tongue from pure emotion, at the thought of your good fortune.'

'Two scythes?'

'Seven and seven. Seventy-seven, in other words, two scythes – if they pass you by without doing you any harm, you're still alive, but from year to year you're bound to keep going downhill, because that's the way of things. And what more can you have to say? And who on earth wants to hear it? If anyone's willing to listen to an old man, he should leave them his fortune. At this age you're simply wondering where the nearest beach is.'

'The nearest beach?'

'Yes, to lie down and start getting used to the sand.'

We're at the New Stage of the National Theatre. Dad admires the foyer. 'Don't forget the *divadlo*,' he kept saying back in Poland, 'that's why we're going in June, to get the best of the *divadlo*, because in July and August the actors are on holiday. Best of all, let's go to the *Národne divadlo* – the National Theatre. We can see some of the others for the buildings, architecture's a wonderful thing, as a builder and decorator I know that. We've got to see as much as possible, son, I like having memories.'

And everything's as it should be, until the ballet begins, a modern one, unfortunately. Israeli and Czech dancers are performing. 'They're jumping about like monkeys' – that's my father's appraisal. It's trance-inducing music, and I'm wondering why on earth I bought tickets for this. We're sitting to one side in the second row, the drums and percussion are thumping away, and noises like drills or refrigerators are raising our blood pressure – you could sue the theatre for ruining your health and win. Mr Gaga, Israel's greatest choreographer, say the reviewers, has prompted the dancers to be guided by a strong primal instinct and they can't resist the movements they're making, but not even I can endure the show, *Decadance*. My father emerges from it feeling mauled. For some time he's too horrified to speak, until at last he says: 'Well, Wifey, son, from now on I'll be on my best behaviour. I promise to be good.'

'Why from now on?' asks Mama.

'Because I don't want to go to hell when I die. And that performance was hell, but it only lasted an hour, not an eternity.'

'One more thing, Dad, you can't start saying in a loud voice that you'd rather have gone to see a play with Zofia Czerwińska during the hush between pieces. The Czechs don't have Zofia Czerwińska, and it's not on to chatter when there's silence on stage.'

'Well, when should I have said it? While they were thumping away at those drums? Who'd have heard me then?'

My parents are having breakfast in their hotel room, and I'm lying on their bed with my laptop. I'm listening to Karel Gott on YouTube, singing 'Forever Young', translated into Czech as 'Být stále mlád'. 'That's a fine thing,' says Dad, 'it was worth coming to Prague just to hear that.' I could explain to him that to me it's an example of an absorbent culture. Czech culture is absorbent. It swallows every foreign body, dissolves it in its gastric juices and processes it into its own pulp. Global Czech hits, for instance. What? You didn't notice, did you? Read it again more slowly! I said 'global Czech hits', but it makes no sense – does it mean the Czechs have produced songs that went global? Not flipping likely! It's just that they Czechify anything and everything, they rewrite every catchy song from English into a Czech version and give it to their own singers to perform. You think you're listening to the Janis Joplin song 'Piece of My Heart', but after a few bars you hear: 'Padni na kolena před jeho laskou...', which sounds all right in Czech, but is quite a shock in Polish.* And

---

* Me again, with the author's consent: the Czech phrase means 'Fall to your knees before his love', but in Polish the word *laska* (the Czech for 'love') sounds like a part of the male anatomy.

the Czech version of 'Killing Me Softly with His Song' is a song about abortion, which says that two little wings are missing in an empty house. And on the radio they're advertising Abba as performed by Hana Zagorová: 'And now,' says the presenter, 'some classic Czech hits!' If a Czech can't customize a word, he won't use it. 'Tolk shaw.' They say 'tolk shaw', and even if I paid seven professional etymologists to work out why, they'd fail. And why do they say 'vikend'? Not 'wikend' with stress on the 'i', but 'vikend' with a distinct 'v' at the start. They've swallowed up the CD and put it out as a *cédéčko* (which sounds like 'se-detch-ko'), and the DVD is a *dívídíčko* (which sounds like 'divvy-ditch-ko'). I saw a drunk on the tram, like a football fan, who stretched out his legs, took out his phone, and said: 'Where are you, Marek, why are you in the car when I'm on the tram? You're right behind the tram? All right, I'll hop off and let's meet at the *K-e-j-e-f-c-iii-č-k-ooo*!' (Yes, that's the K-F-C-itch-ko.)

Dad, I'll tell you what this weird phenomenon is. It's patriotism! A show of patriotism – that's what love of your homeland is all about. Love of your own culture – because the Czechs have always believed that the person who publishes a dictionary will do more good for their grandchildren than the rebel who brandishes a pistol. When he gave lectures in Paris, the great Polish poet Adam Mickiewicz declared that a Czech intellectual may be industrious, but he can't distinguish a vital aim from a trivial one. It'd only be vital if he were prepared to have a fight. But the Poles who travelled through the Czech lands in the nineteenth century reported that the nation was in moral decline because it wasn't inciting insurgencies. But I, as a twenty-first-century traveller, can see the moral superiority inherent in *Kejefcičko*, ladies and gentlemen.

'Do they have tonic at the whatsitchko?' asks Dad.

In the hot June weather here in Prague, Dad has been discovering tonic water. Until now he has never tolerated anything but tea and the dishes Mama learned to make in the mid-twentieth century when they got married. Offered Coca-Cola in Warsaw, he says he tried it once, just after leaving the army, and no thank you very much. In Prague he's open to everything, even drinks that aren't tea.

So two scythes have passed him by and he's having his first taste of tonic, warm, because he can't bear anything cold, mixed with still water. We go into various cafés and order it. 'If, as you say, this is a cubist café and it's one hundred years old, perhaps the tonic here will taste sharper, seeing cubism has such sharp corners? Heh heh heh!' 'Dad, the reason why Prague has such interesting architecture from a hundred years ago is because the Czechs and the Germans fought each other.' 'The Czechs fought the Germans, did you say? When was that?' 'Yes, but the fight was in architecture – if a German family built an interesting house, a Czech family built an even more interesting one. And that's how avant-garde Prague came into being. And the houses built by the Czechs are very surprising – they didn't have a state of their own, but they did conspire, through construction. Take cubism – the houses were meant to look as if they were moving, as if they were vibrating. They reckoned it was already such a resonant, dynamic era, the year 1913, that a cubist house had to reflect those unsettled times by vibrating.'

'Tell me, son, when's Franz Kafka?'

'Franz Kafka?' I'm gobsmacked. 'Why are you so surprised? You know it all but you've never heard the words "Franz" and "Kafka" before?' 'But what do you want with Franz Kafka, Dad?' 'What do you mean? When I could still see well, I read that he lived at his sister's place on Golden Lane, at number twenty-two, apparently, but they can't have got on well, because he moved out. That probably suited him better, a man should be independent. We went there once, didn't we? And I'd like to see that tiny house where they lived again.'

'Why do you want to see it again?'

'To fix it in my mind. Some things should be fixed in the mind, son. Then a person might dream about them, for instance. When he's lost his sight entirely.'

EWA'S BALANCE SHEET

The most interesting stories appear out of the blue. They don't announce: 'Now I'm going to reveal myself and be an absolute delight!' If it's brazen enough to forecast its arrival, to send heralds in advance and beat on drums, it's usually disappointing. 'I've got a great story for you, please come by.' I feel as if I were going to see a prostitute, and yet I go. Anyone who's made of more than just flesh soon feels the need to fill their spiritual void.

The most interesting stories don't know they're the most interesting. They need help. They need a medic to confirm: 'It's on its way, madam!' They need a midwife to cut the umbilical cord.

So one of the most interesting stories turned up while we were eating chicken and rice with salad.

No.	YEAR		SUCCESSES	FAILURES	STRESS
			Data from documents		
1	1950	Other	06.11 – born in Świdnica		
2			26.11 – baptism certificate no. xxx/1950		
	1957				Dad's funeral
					Family & financial problems
3	1959	Other	First communion		Missed 24 days in Form II (no excuse given)
					Move to Upper Silesia
	1960				Missed 27 days in Form III
4	1961	Other	23.09 – confirmation in Tychy		Family & financial problems
28	1967	Media	First ballet performance in my life, *The Fountain of Bakhchisarai*		Family & financial problems
29		Other	Correspondence with Japanese penfriend Takato, until 1968 (two gifts)		Quarantine at boarding school – scabies
30			Letter from Japanese friend Akitomo ('Radar')		
31			Triple sanatorium stay in Ciechocinek		
32			4th place for 'Turkish woman' at the carnival ball at the Mining and Economics Technical College		
33			Expedition to Kraków and the Pieniny Range		
34			Started my housing savings book		
42	1969	Other	High-school graduation exams – catering technician; writing out certificates in Forms IV & V		Family & financial problems
43			Entrance exams for college in Katowice (Faculty of Trade and Food Technology)		Decision re studies
44			Change of work placement location to Ustroń-Jaszowiec – Voluntary Labour Corps at the City Enterprise for Communal Economy – 850 zlotys		
45			ZMS [Union of Socialist Youth] integration camp at Wilkasy – ritual baptism of Neptune and acceptance into the student brotherhood (nickname: Lame Oyster)		
46			ZSP [Polish Students' Association] member until 1973		
47			AZS [Academic Sports Association] member until 1973		
48			Friendship with A.K. until 1970		
52			Work experience in forestry nr. Giszowiec		

			Data from pocket diary	
59	1972	Media	Theatrical Meetings – Silesian Theatre, Katowice	
60			Reply from sociologist Mikołaj Kozakiewicz (M.R.)	Financial problems
61		Other	Economic theory exam – v.g.	
62			35th anniversary of WSE [Katowice Academy of Economics] – Ekonomalia '72	
63			Vice-Chancellor's Award, average >4.43	
64			Member of the 'Skarbek' Student Labour Cooperative until 1973	
65			Member of the artistic gymnastics division – two terms, offer of dean's leave (championships)	
66			Winter school camp, ZU [College Administration Office], ZMS in Wisła for free	
67			KNEŻ (food economics study group) expedition – Warsaw, and KNEŻ camp – Bielsko-Biała	
70	1973		First trip abroad to Germany (2nd prize for KNEŻ paper)	
71			Ekonomalia '73	
72			Member of SZSP [Socialist Union of Polish Students]	
73			International work camp in Hungary – 3 weeks in Budapest, 10 days' leisure on Lake Balaton	
74			PTTK [Polish Tourist & Sightseeing Society] GOT [Mountain Tourist badge] – bronze	
75			Correspondence with Czech Janos until 1974	
76			Correspondence with Bulgarian Ivan until 1974	Move to Opole
77			Member of TKKF [Society for the Promotion of Physical Culture] Hearth Club, Opole	First professional work – at OZKS [Opole Food Concentrate Plant], financial problems
78			Member of the Professional Union of Workers in the Food and Sugar Industry until 1977	
79			Member of the Opole Housing Cooperative 'Przyszłość'	
80			Provisional flat allocation	
81	1974	Other	Cooperative flat allocation	Financial problems, two loans
82			Friendship with S.S. (ballet Swan Lake in Wrocław)	
83			Graduation ceremony at WSE Katowice	
84			Member of Wektory social dance group	
96	1977	TKKF	20th anniversary of TKKF Hearth Club Opole	
97			Honourable TKKF badge 'For Services to Disseminating Physical Recreation' (ZW [Provincial Office] Opole)	
98		Other	G. from Kępa's parents' 25th wedding anniversary	Change of job, move to WSS
99			Portrait of a Girl, painting by my grandfather Edward Karniej at 'The Woman in Polish Painting' exhibition at BWA Opole [Art Exhibitions Bureau]	
100			Legacy from H., approx. 700 zlotys	

114	1981	Other	'Friendship Train' expedition to the USSR with Gromada [Nationwide Tourist Cooperative] – 416 people (Minsk, Moscow, Leningrad, Vilnius)		Ration cards for meat, butter and cereal
115			S.S.'s visit	Broke up with Z.R.	
116			12.12 – gathering of graduates of WSE Katowice employed at Opole district workplaces		
123	1986	TKKF	Course for instructors running exercise classes for the elderly – Zakopane		
151	1993	TKKF	20th anniversary of activity at TKKF Hearth Club Opole		
152			Secretary of TKKF Hearth Club Opole		
153		Media	Summer opera meetings on TV Polonia 1, autographed photo from La Scala director Riccardo Muti		
154			Three descriptions in *Super Express*		
155			One description in *Flirt*		
156			One description in 'Wings', *Express Wieczorny*		
157		Other	Correspondence with Jadzia from PHS [Food Trade Enterprise], continues to this day		Financial problems
167	1996	PTTK	Member of PTTK in Opole		
168			Member of board of PTTK Circle No. 16		
169			Two descriptions in 'Wings', *Express Wieczorny* ('Personal Ten Commandments' and 'Writing Instils Habits')		
170			Prize from Radio Opole		
171			Prize for 50th anniversary of *Express Wieczorny*		
172			Two prizes from *Super Express* (one for droodles in *Gilotyn*)		
173			Issue of *Teleexpress* (concert for glass bells at Opole Philharmonic)		
174		Media	Reply from actor Jan Matyjaszkiewicz from the Ateneum Theatre, Warsaw (numerology)		
175			Trip to Hungary with Karlik (Danube bend, Budapest)		
176		Other	Diploma 'for sense of humour and promoting positive thinking among fellow workers'		
177			Correspondence with Maria from Florida and Belgium (after my letter to *Express Wieczorny*), until 2004		Financial problems
196	1999	PTTK	Treasurer for PTTK Circle No. 16		
197		Media	Letter, 'Being a Soloist is Nothing', in *Wysokie Obcasy*		
198			Three broadcasts by Edward Spyrka, *My Concert*, on Radio Opole live (Riccardo Muti)		
199		Other	Coach trip to Paris and Rheims with Almatur		
200			Online meeting after many years with cousin Basia		Postgraduate studies
201			Treasurer for postgraduate studies group – 2 terms		Financial problems

No.	Year	Category	Description		Notes
226	2003	PTTK	GOT badge, small silver		
227			Congratulatory diploma from ZG (Head Office), PTTK Warsaw ('for services to the promotion of tourism and sightseeing')		
228			40th anniversary of PTTK Circle No. 16		
230		TKKF	30th anniversary of TKKF Hearth Club Opole		
232		Other	Weekend trip to the Czech Republic with Almatur (Kutná Hora, Prague, Karlovy Vary), prize from Opole Philharmonic		Colonoscopy
233			Diploma for 30th anniversary of professional work	No wage rise	Financial problems
264	2007	PTTK	GOT badge: level II, 'For stamina'		
265			GOT badge: level III, 'For stamina'		
266			Walker's badge, small silver		
267			Delegate at Extraordinary Assembly Opole PTTK		
268			Accepted for Conquerors of Summits of Polish Mountains Club, no. xxxx		
269		TKKF	Secretary of Board of TKKF Hearth Club, Opole		Funeral of H.M., chair of TKKF Hearth Club, Opole
272		Media	Prize in contest for election slogan in Gazeta Wyborcza ('Poles Can Do It! And That Includes Voting!')		
273			Conversation with and autograph from Jan Milun (musician, opera singer and promotor of Polish music in the USA, awarded the George Washington medal)		
275		Other	Became reacquainted with quality controllers at PHS		K.K.'s funeral
276			Became reacquainted with Ala		Illness and death of Harald
277			My will – leaving my flat to a child from children's home in C.		Resigned from group function at U3A swimming pool
278			Breaking the record for open-air gymnastics, approx. 1,000 people, hosted by Wyborcza (Owsiak)		
339	2012	PTTK	'Eagle's Nest Trail' badge		
340			'Lover of the Jura' 'Popular' bronze badge		
341			GOT badge: level VIII, 'For stamina'		
342			'I Know the History of the Technology Trail, Silesian District' badge		
343			International 'Beskydy' Beskid Range badge – 3 countries (Poland, Czech Republic and Slovakia)		
344			Thank you from the Opole District Marshal (Opole Tourism Days 2012)		
345			Secretary for 'Ride with Baba'		
346			8 hikes for social work		

347	2012		20 hike descriptions on the PTTK Opole website		
348			Trip to Albania with J.M. Travel Agency		
349			Trip to Bohemian Switzerland (Pravčická Gate)		
350			Expedition to the Pieniny Range for tourism organizers		
351			Night-time New Year's Eve party on Biskupia Kopa, 889 m		
353		Media	Winner of Opole Philharmonic photography competition		
355			1 description on www.jestemwformie.pl website		
356			Dance workshops at Student Cultural Centre (autograph of Iwona Pavlović)		
358			Photo from Albania + autograph of photographer Chris Niedenthal (II Opole Festival of Photography)		
359		Other	Reactivation of Skorpion Club (pensioners)	Broke up with R.R.	Mammogram, USG, MRI. Cracked knee, twisted elbow joint
360			Two certificates from Podbiegi (I & II Open Opole Citizens' Pacing and Running)		
411	2015	PTTK	7 descriptions of expeditions for PTTK Opole		
412			'Crown of the Sudety Range' badge		
413			'Polish–Czech Borderland Mountains' badge		
414			Small PTTK Vistula Tourist badge		
415			'Lower Silesian Tourist' silver badge		
416			For my 65th birthday climbed Kasprowy Wierch – 1,987 m, starting from Toporowa Cyrla – 992 m		
417			28/28 peaks for the Crown of Polish Mountains		
418		Media	17 photos of Paris in the 'France Through the Lens of Opole Citizens' exhibition at the WBP [provincial public library] (organized by the Foreign Language Library)		
419			5 photos in photography exhibition at the PROvince Museum in Głogowek (the world's most consumer exhibition – 'Show 5 Things That Are Important to You': Muti, portrait of grandmother...)		
421			Meeting with Prime Minister Ewa Kopacz organized by 'Senior-WIGOR' programme		Went to see the doctor at U.'s
423			Zumba at DDP Magda-Maria [day centre], from January		
424			Social dance at Novomex – 5 classes		
425			Salsa solo at Royal Dance Centre – 4 months, certificate		
426			6 Zumba shows and a fashion show		
427			'Logographs on the Move' project – dance workshops and show on improvised movement, at GSW [modern art gallery]		

#	Year	Category	Description
428	2015		Mobile choir at GSW, from September
429			Participated in video made by Nina from Karlsruhe
430			Latino dance at Salsa Fuerte – 3 classes
431		Various	Diploma for completing Young Hearts Academy – 1 year
433			Debut – role of Devil at Christmas Fair
465	2017	PTTK	5 hike descriptions on PTTK Opole website
466			Bronze badge, 'Trails of Wooden Churches in the Opole Region'
467			Silver Regional Sightseeing badge
468			'Popular' badge, 'On the Trail of UNESCO World Heritage Sites in Poland'
469			Bronze badge, 'On the Trail of UNESCO World Heritage Sites in Poland'
470			Silver badge, 'On the Trail of UNESCO World Heritage Sites in Poland'
471			Small gold Hiking badge
472			Wałbrzych County badge
473			Wałbrzych County badge 'For stamina'
474			Gold badge, 'Lower Silesia Tourist'
475			Grade 3 badge, 'Senior Tourist'
476			60/80 peaks in the Polish Mountains Diadem
478		Media	FB – review of film *Last Tango* on day of premiere, 17.02, in profile 'Spectator – more than cinema'
479			Two photos at 'Urban Legends' exhibition at MŚO [Opole Silesian Museum]
480			50+ fashion show during Opole Days!! + interview for www.24Opole.pl
485			5 Zumba shows in Opole + 1 in Pakosławice + 1 in Nysa + 1 in Kędzierzyn-Koźle
486			Diploma and statuette for taking part in Dance Festival in Pakosławice
487			Photo with choreographer Jaime Pablo Diaz (Nova Galeria de Danza)
488			Won contest for advertising slogan 'Spain in Opole...'
489			Casting for mock documentary series (Studio Wrocław)
490			Two operas live, *Rigoletto* and *Nabucco*
492			Theatre workshops for seniors at Opole Puppet and Actors' Theatre – photo in *Opole i Kropka* monthly
493			'Opole Citizens' Self-Portrait' project – film entitled *Picture in the Phone*
494			Conversation and photo with cameraman Sławomir Idziak
495			Recording for 'director of life' – 3 questions

496	2017		
498		Various	Last, 296th, film (over 7 years) at Library Film Club, *The Best of Everything* Diploma for completing Young Hearts Academy – 3rd year
499			Discovery of the year – agent among friends Christmas & New Year holiday, Kudowa-Zdrój

'Take a look: so far I've got 504 successes, 17 failures and 93 stresses. This is the Excel table of my life.'

'Well, there have to be more successes.'

'There have to be. I simply have no alternative.'

'Fewer stresses, because I'm good at watching out for them.'

'That's because I'm meticulous. I remember the dates that have to be remembered. You could call me an accountant. I graduated in economics, but I've never actually worked in bookkeeping.'

'It doesn't hurt, accountancy is second nature to me.'

'My earliest memories? They're of Świdnica. We lived near the city centre, there was a shop on the ground floor. Now it's a dog-grooming parlour. I wasn't yet seven, and my parents had sent me to get two quarter bottles of vodka. I carried them under my arms and climbed to the fourth floor. I had trouble opening the door, one of the bottles fell from my grip and broke.'

'A pleasant childhood memory? The fact Dad didn't beat me for breaking that bottle.'

'How they sold me the vodka I have no idea. I know for sure I wasn't seven yet. Because at the age of seven I found my dad dead. On the third of October, I came home from school, went into the living room, and saw my father lying across the bed, and a puddle on the floor. I touched him, and he was all cold. Why was it me who had to find my father's dead body?'

'I only discovered the meaning of it later on.'

'All these years have gone by, but I can still remember the sense of rejection. I've forgotten who took the little group of kids to the market garden. At the end of the visit the gardener gave each child a flower, but there wasn't one for me – the only kid who didn't get one.'

'Perhaps it was my appearance? My modest clothing?'

'In the living room a picture by my granddad, who was a painter, hung in pride of place. I remember whom it portrayed: a naked girl with a jug on her head, on her way to a spring. In adult life I found out what the critics wrote about him: "Edward Karniej was a master of the nude form, especially of light on the naked female body." When did that picture disappear from the wall and get drunk away? I have no idea where it is now – it could be in a gallery, a museum or a private house. I have no mementoes of my granddad, but I might have had.'

'You're right, the light seems to slide across those women's bodies.'

'My father was rarely at home, so my memories of him are foggy. I remember a time when he worked as a lorry driver. Apparently he was handsome. When I look at photos of him I can see that he was. And when I look at the portrait of him painted by his brother, Henryk – that one of my granddad's sons was a painter too – I think it's the face of a strong, handsome man. But he must have been weak. Strong men don't drink. My mother claimed that when she looked down from our fourth-floor window and saw him walking along the pavement, she felt like jumping out.'

'Maybe she felt unappreciated in that relationship? Maybe she felt inferior? Wanting to throw herself out of the window is a sign of my mum's destructive behaviour, which got worse later on in Upper Silesia.'

'I wasn't the only child of that marriage. My sister Basia was two years old when she died of meningitis. And I was four at the time. Why did I have to keep hearing how lovely Basia was, with her black hair and blue eyes? After all, I was very similar to her, and unlike her, I was still alive. It appears from the documents that in the second year at junior school I missed twenty-four days of lessons, but no excuse was recorded. I can't remember being ill for that long, so what happened to me?'

'I have absolutely no memory of that.'

'In October 1959, just before my ninth birthday, my mother announced that she was leaving the city and taking me back to Upper Silesia, to her family in Tychy. She literally descended on them. Ignoring the fact that we were leaving our flat in Świdnica behind, and that I was settled at school. She never went back to Świdnica again, she never visited my father's grave, and I was automatically deprived of contact with his family.'

'The new flat was just a living room and a kitchen. My mother and I slept in the kitchen with my uncle, who was also a drunk. My grandmother, aunt and her daughter slept in the living room. There was no harmony between us. And both my grandmother and aunt had an aversion to me. To them I was just that dipso woman's daughter. I could sense it every step of the way. My grandmother would buy buns for my cousin, but I never attained this honour. A few years later life in the flat became less fraught, because my grandmother died, and my aunt and cousin got a place in a new block. My uncle went on living in the kitchen, while my mother and I occupied the main room. Better, you'd think, but... When they renovated the building, all the residents got running water and a WC in their flats, except for us. You had to contribute some money to the renovation, but here it all went on booze. As a result, I used to walk to the well for water, and we had an outhouse in the yard. The flat wasn't heated, you had to pay for coal, but the money went on drink. I used to sleep in my clothes, and in later years I could never cope with having cold hands and feet in winter. I wanted to be top of the class, but I could never fully succeed. I'll give you an example. We were set a homework assignment: "Force a bean to sprout." How can you do that in a cold flat?'

'It was so cold that not even a runner bean wanted to live at our place.'

'Another example: the lack of personal hygiene. I remember my humiliation at a PE lesson. We had to walk along a balance beam barefoot. And I heard someone comment: "What dirty feet she has." I slept in my clothes, and I very rarely had access to hot water. My mother never soiled her hands with work, nor did my uncle. What a pair of scroungers! Why go to work when there's the family pension left by my father. The postman used to deliver the money to the house, but to get it faster, my mother would force me to go to the post office with her and lie in wait for the postman. The upshot was that for the first few days I had to ration out the money to my mother. But all I ever heard was "Give me, give me," and the pension was soon gone. But life teaches us to be resourceful. I had a navy-blue pleated skirt, the kind you wear to school, and I unstitched the waistband, put the banknotes in there and secured them with a safety pin. No one could detect it.

'One time, our neighbour on the second floor, who had a gas cylinder and made balloons, took me to a New Year's Eve party.'

'No. So I'd help him to sell those balloons. And I was in a shiny school pinafore. I felt dreadfully ashamed. But I wanted to have at least a little bit of money for myself. Utter humiliation, but all worth it to get hold of a few banknotes. I went home at dawn, and they let me sleep in a bit, but then the nagging began: "Give me, give me!" All three of them: my mother, my uncle, and her pal from the dump...'

'From the rubbish dump. When there was no money left for drink, my mother would go to the dump, and pick up waste paper and bottles. For company she had this fellow of the same type as her, and I had to spend my time in this extended company. Afterwards I had to wash the bottles, and the stink was awful. It was a long way to the purchasing centre where they paid for recycling material, so you had to take the bus. I used to go with her, it was really crowded, and when the time came to get off I'd hear her shriek at the top of her voice: "Ewa, we're getting off." The bottles would clink and clank, and my shame would go sky high. My mother used to drink with the rubbish-dump man and she slept with him too. I remember a scene, stripped of all romance. Where on earth could I go? My uncle was in the kitchen, and the three of us were in the main room. He was lying on top of her, heaving away to get the job done, and she was smoking a cigarette in a holder, staring cynically at the ceiling, wondering when the guy would finally get off her. Why can't I wipe that image from memory? If only I had some little keys, I'd lock up those memories and never go back to them. It's as if the memory is a fortress, there you stand in its courtyard, but you can't leave because the keys to the gate are on the outside.'

'Oh yes. All three of them – my mum, the man and my uncle – hung over me like vultures. "Give me! Give me!" That'd make a fine scene in a movie, but a bit horrifying. I was afraid they might do something to me. I handed it all over to them.'

'I used to escape from my mother, literally. In front of the house there was a little piece of garden, with a few trees and some grass. One of the trees stood by a fence, and Irka from the first floor and I used to climb it. Whenever my mother came home pie-eyed, that was my hiding place. Sometimes she knew where I was, so she'd stand underneath the tree and yammer away as loud as she could. But I'd be at the top!'

'There was a nice moment too. One Sunday she sent me to the cinema to watch the morning show for kids. I was terribly amazed: I was at the cinema! There was a surprise waiting for me when I got home, because she was lying on the bed after a dose of some pills washed down with alcohol. I raced off to the emergency department, because there was no phone at home. We drove back in an ambulance, I was quite incapable of speech, all I could do was point which way to go. They brought her round. All those times she woke me at dawn, and I saw a hatchet above my head, and I had those racing thoughts: will it fall or not? Or those offers of hers: set the alarm for six a.m., we'll go to the tracks and under a train.'

'So why did this happen to me? There's no answer, I've nowhere to lodge a complaint and nobody to hear it.'

'I used to think: "When will I finally see light at the end of the tunnel?" I was a good student. I had my place of refuge – the library. Thanks to social services I ended up at a boarding school. It was one of the caregivers, rather than my mother, who took me to the technical college entrance exam. You had to pay for the boarding school. Those ladies came up with a brilliant idea. They realized that the children's home could pay, and my only obligation would be to apply myself to my studies. A fabulous idea, and both sides met their obligations. But I realized I had to repay the debt.'

'Well, I regard it as a debt. That's why I wrote my will. My little flat will be given to a child from the children's home. It's not far from here, in a place just outside Opole.'

'I remember the look on my mother's face when I let it slip that I'd started a housing savings book for myself when I was still at middle school. Her face was priceless. The contributions weren't huge, and I was putting something away for college too, but that savings book helped me a great deal in getting allocated a cooperative flat. How many times did I hear them say "You'll never get by in life"?'

'Yes, of course I sometimes think well of my mum. I've adopted the view of a wise woman who once said that a mother is not someone you can rely on, but someone who teaches you how to get by without having to rely on others. Perhaps my mum wasn't aware of what she was doing, but as a result I get by in life without support! Do you know, I once generated virtual gravestones for my parents, and that's the idea behind it?'

'That's because in my youth I was a bit of a peeping Tom.'

'A psychological peeping Tom. I sought out traits that I liked in people and that might suit me. I'd wonder whether I could adopt those traits. With some modification, a bit of work on myself, I shaped a new Ewa.'

'For example, the woman who ran the boarding school, outwardly a virago, but thanks to her I began to take care of my personal hygiene, go to the theatre and to concerts. Or my maths teacher. In my second year at the college I visited her at home. It was December, I was very badly dressed and I was cold. And early in January I received a package from her: a pair of woollen socks she had knitted for me, and the rest of the ball of yarn, in case of holes. I've been repaying that debt too: I correspond with her daughter. In short, I owe a lot to others who aren't my relatives.'

'Applying a "surgical cut" was a brilliant solution. I didn't know where I'd end up after college, and for two and a half years after Mum's death I went on paying the rent for that flat where my drunkard of an uncle was still living. I didn't want to go back to where I was from. I changed region, literally everything. A surgical cut of this kind is an excellent solution as long as it's a well-thought-out move, without a shadow of doubt.'

'You can't have any doubts, or it won't work. It really was a headlong dive without knowing how to swim, but I came up to the surface. I started off in Opole with a single teaspoon. I remember the early days, after being allocated a flat in a block. The sun peeped in through the windowpanes, the whole place was empty, except for a chair-bed, a stool borrowed from a lady in my faculty, bedding also borrowed from my workplace, and a few things of my own in old bulk bags, set against the wall. And I felt proud. The only problem I had was with divulging the details of my life.'

'Well, what can you tell new acquaintances about yourself? Who can I say I am? Why am I not in touch with my family? Who are your parents, Ewa? Being too frank can bring about a sudden drop in your ratings among others, you know?'

'Nowadays? I'm not at all afraid to be judged. Americans say you can't judge someone until you've walked a mile in their shoes.'

'On the TV set, to the left? A conductor. That's proof that the guy who conducts the orchestra at La Scala can give wings to a woman in Opole.'

'Pick it up. He's written "Per Eva con simpatia – Riccardo Muti". How beautifully he turns a phrase... He dances with his baton... On 2 June 1995, his orchestra went on strike and he replaced it all by himself. He accompanied the singers on the piano for the whole of *La Traviata*!'

'I saw him on television in the early 1990s. I decided to write him a letter. I couldn't find the address of La Scala, but I found a translator into Italian and it all got much easier. I remember queuing at the post office with that letter, my back dripping with sweat, as I said to myself: "Ewa, what on earth are you up to?" In less than seven weeks I got an answer! A photo with a dedication and an autograph. Right on my forty-second birthday! "What can I send him in return?" I thought. I chose a post-card of a rose on a grand piano. More than twenty years have passed since then, but I've kept up the tradition of sending him birthday greetings. He always writes back! Afterwards I wrote to the Italian Cultural Institute in Warsaw to ask if they knew the dates of his professional anniversary. They didn't, but they sent me his private address. He lives in Ravenna. I was amazed because you don't give out the addresses of famous people. I wondered whether it was appropriate to write to him at that address. I wrote to our local paper to ask for advice.'

'Well, I had no one to advise me. I've always been self-reliant and I had to find a solution by myself.'

'They gave me an answer on their letters page, saying that if I wanted to observe strict etiquette, I should continue to write to the theatre address. But as life can't be straitjacketed by inflexible rules, they advised me to take advantage of the opportunity I'd been given. Especially since he was addressing me as "Gentile Eva" by now, meaning "Dear Ewa", which showed we were on familiar terms. But they said I should mention that I got the address from the institute. In fact, I didn't take advantage of the private address. A few days later I was at work and someone said: "Ewa, the deputy director wants to see you." I was so scared, my hair stood on end. The deputy director asked if I was the person who'd written to the newspaper. And our whole conversation was about going to the philharmonic and music, because the deputy director was a music lover too. The upshot was that he sent me off for postgraduate studies.'

'Yes. Aged over forty, as a company employee, I did postgraduate studies at the Academy of Economics in Wrocław, in bookkeeping and auditing.'

'Unfortunately not, but I did look for a conductor who could to some extent be my substitute for him in Poland. I found one in Kraków, but his name will remain my sweet secret. Such masterly expression! In the interval, I went to his dressing room to get his autograph. I peeped in and saw him lying down, hardly breathing, wiping the sweat from his brow, though moments ago he'd been storming away on stage. "Ewa," I said to myself, "back off." But if I hadn't tried, I'd have been upset with myself. There's a kind of person who has the sort of life where they have to learn a special art.'

'Didn't I say? They have to learn to take pleasure in the small, trivial things. Because they have no alternative.'

'No, I've got the other conductor's autograph now, I've even got a photograph of us together. One of my friends, who's very fond of me, wanted to give me a present, so he told the conductor he had a loyal fan who didn't have his autograph. Suddenly, I got a lovely email from the conductor and I was invited to the philharmonic. To hear Grieg and Rachmaninov.'

'"Ewa," they say, "writing letters to a conductor isn't life." To which I reply: "Emotions, my dear friends, emotions are life!"'

'What makes an event count as a success? Let me think...'

'Ah, a success to be written down in the Excel table. My life's greatest success is keeping my joie de vivre, which is made up of lots of the tiny little successes I've recorded.'

'I think we achieve success once we're ready for it in every way: spiritual, emotional and even physical. My episode with

Riccardo Muti could only start in 1993. Before then it wouldn't have been possible, I wasn't ready for it.'

'Yes, that's right. I wasn't ready to write the letter. Only after listening to x number of symphonies, reading x number of books about music and gaining greater self-confidence could I say to myself: "Ewa, now you can afford that." I uphold the theory that each event in life is bound to take place at a precisely determined time. We have to be suitably prepared and to be aware that we've done everything for this success to take place. As Plato said, the most important part of any action is the start. And as a result, we reap what we sow. That's Epictetus.'

'I got out of my own life story? I escaped from my own life story? I'll make a note of that: *Things* by Georges Perec.'

'I knew you'd ask: why the Excel table?'

'I told you at the beginning that it's the Excel table of my life. A trusted neighbour has the key to my flat. I can very much rely on him. But will he be the first to enter? I don't know. What if it's a policeman? Or a fireman who breaks down the door? In any case, I'm counting on the fact that whoever goes in will see the body, and my laptop will be open on the desk with the Excel table. And that person will take a look at it.

'And say: "That's how Ewa lived."'

A HAT FOR THE WORLD

A son reads a long sentence written by Ludwik Adam Jucewicz in 1842: 'Yielding to the throng of reminiscences preserved in our minds, together we would like to fathom this vast mass and impress its stamp on our memory; but when we start to apply thought, with cold consideration, most of the objects disappear from our attention.'

The son goes on leafing through the pages of *Metaphors of Memory* by Grzegorz Marzec, which he has just been given as a present by a friend, and his eyes light on the words of Julian Ursyn Niemcewicz, printed for the first time in 1868: 'So everyone eagerly grabs hold of works that double their existence by uniting the past and the present time.'

The son suddenly comes to the conclusion that his father, who is losing his memory, and whose sight is going on top of that, hasn't yet been memorialized. The world must remember his father. His first association is the slogan 'The Internet Remembers!'

The son explains to his eighty-five-year-old father what the internet is. 'We'll be gone, but the internet will still be there. Quite simply, Dad, it'll always be there!' The father protests that only God is always going to be there. 'All right, the internet will be there until the end of electricity.'

The father says: 'I know something about electricity, a house painter and decorator needs to know that sort of thing.'

The son explains to his father that he's going to record a short video of him and take his picture. He asks his father to say where he feels at his best. That's where they'll perform the act of immortalizing him. 'In your study,' says the father, 'I'm happy in there.'

The son invites his father over. They divide the process into two meetings, because the father wants to be in different outfits for the video and for the photograph.

First the father puts on a green pullover. Once the iPhone video recording is underway, the son asks his father what he thinks about when he's in his son's study.

The father replies: 'Well, son, you know how to talk to books. Because you have to know how to talk to books.'

The next day the father – about to be immortalized in his second outfit too – comes to pose for his photograph. He's wearing a hat. It's white with thin blue stripes.

As soon as he comes in, the father has a dilemma. 'In the first place, son, I can't be photographed in a hat, because it's not appropriate to sit indoors in headgear, but I can't be photographed without it either, because that's the whole charm of it. What's more, it's an Italian hat from Sardinia. Maybe do it so that I'm turning to the ladies and gentlemen and tipping my hat to them by way of greeting. Then everyone will be satisfied.'

Now the father is lying on the couch on which his son reads books. Because that's his favourite place in his favourite room at his son's flat. He's looking at the wall. 'That painting is too grey,' he says (about a picture by Filip Černý, which is also on the cover of one of the books written by the son). The father has an idea: 'I'd add some green leaves to those grey and black flowers. And I'd do it nicely, because I'm an artistic painter and decorator.'

The son explains that the Czech artist may have had a different idea in mind. For example, some people might be in a mental state where they see flowers only as grey or black.

The father is quick to provide a riposte: 'There, you see, you know about people, and I know about painting.'

The son posts the picture of his father on Instagram, in which he's touching his hat from Sardinia with his right hand. Next day, the photo has 1,752 likes and 105 comments.

People write that they love their own fathers, that they no longer have their fathers, and even that they love that son's father.

The son gets his mother to read the comments aloud.

On a Sunday afternoon, the mother reads out the comments and says she can't understand why there's so much interest in the father.

Feeling happy, the father makes sure: 'So now I'm in the history of the world, am I?'

THE CORRECT COLUMN

I realized a sad thing: Ewa, who keeps the Excel table of her life, won't be able to complete it herself. Fill in the final entry.

I wrote to her to say that.

'That's a valid point,' she replied. 'I've thought about it, and I've come up with a solution. I'll leave a short message for the person who comes upon my Excel table. In it I'll write, would they please be sure to add the date of my death to the "Successes" column.

'I'll explain why.

'If someone else were going to enter my death in the "Failures" column, there's only one circumstance in which they could do it – and that's if, on my death bed, in so far as I could do any thinking in that situation, I thought: "At last! I'm a frustrated, unhappy woman and it's a good thing I'm leaving this vale of tears." But as you know, Mr Szczygieł, that's not true. You've been observing me for the past six months, ever since we met, and you're sure to agree with me that in my case it will only be a success.

'Life itself is a success, so its ending is too!

'Have a good day,

'Ewa.'

CLEARANCE

A middle-aged woman, not particularly fancy, or visibly self-important in any way.

She's standing at the librarian's desk.

She's looking for some specific books, and – to those in the queue behind her – this betrays her secret.

What occurs to me is that she's looking for a place to hide.

She tells the lady librarian she'd like to take another look at her favourite books from childhood. I assume she's hoping to hide in them. The magic of the written word lies in the fact that it creates images. Literature, wrote Jan Parandowski, is governed by a time that's different from the kind that regulates everyday life, and even from the kind that moves the hands on the clock of history. In literature the past, the present and the future are not delineated by a simple order, they haven't any limits of their own, but flow in a common, uniform stream. So when a middle-aged woman asks for books from the time when she was a girl, it also occurs to me that she'd like to jump into them and jump out on the other side. Into her youth, which is still going on.

She takes a piece of paper from her handbag. She shows the specific titles, but the librarian can't find them.

'No books by any of these writers?' says the woman, dismayed.

The librarian finally comes upon... one of them!

'You've saved it from its doom,' she says.

'From its doom?' we all wonder in the queue.

'We're just about to start clearance. Nothing can save the books that nobody borrows.'

The librarian picks up the book and whispers to it tenderly: 'You see, my dear, you've escaped selection, you're going to go on living.'

'Selection?'

The librarian looks at us, amazed.

'Of course. We withdraw the books that are very battered or scribbled on, have missing pages or are obsolete. But we also have an obligation to eliminate books that aren't read. The ones that haven't been borrowed for ten years. And there are some libraries where if no one touches a book for just five years its fate is sealed.'

'And then what happens to it?'

'We tear out the pages with the library stamps and then send the withdrawn books for recycling. A receipt from the recycling centre is attached to the clearance record to prove the paper has been reused. But please don't laugh, those are the rules.'

We're not laughing, quite the opposite.

'But how can you have the heart to withdraw a book that's on the shelf?' asks the librarian.

'My heart would break,' says the woman who's come in search of her youth.

'The so-called guiding authorities expect us to do some clearance every year. To show that the collection is alive. We buy something, and we throw something away. But how do we assign a book to clearance? Usually we choose the ones of which we have several copies, then the authorities are satisfied, and the librarian's heart remains intact. Libraries usually make their selection for a more prosaic reason – a lack of space for new purchases. In the past these withdrawals were displayed on a shelf and sold for a so-called "zloty to buy the librarian a pencil". I've never used arguments for clearance like "The book wasn't being read" or "The book's not in the canon." I believe that every single book might be needed by someone… I have a psychological problem with this. It's a lesson I grew up with – we don't throw away bread or books. I should stress that, in any given year, the library can't withdraw more books than it has bought. Right now, I'm selecting those published in the 1960s and 1970s, so you're bang on target with the authors on your list.'

The librarian hands the woman the rescued book.

Something banal and obvious occurs to me: words are not a reflection of reality. The term 'clearance'! Designed to magic the facts into being something else. Not 'incineration', not 'disposal', not 'destruction', but 'clearance'. A word devoid of emotion.

The woman sits down at a small table and skims the book. Suddenly, she puts it in her handbag and says: 'Well, so I was lucky, goodbye,' and leaves, smiling to herself.

A PRESENTIMENT

... I have both Arctic wars at my fingertips. I've written down everything we need to know about them, and my wife Joanna has recorded it. I'll send you a link, she reads very nicely, she's a television reporter, so she's skilled.

...Yes, a highly professional voice, thanks to which the Arctic wars sound completely real.

...And why shouldn't there be a war? There will be a war. After each war they always say there'll never be another, but there always is.

...Because the climate will get hotter, the ice will melt and wars will break out over the Arctic...

...Yes, I have one child, a daughter, Zuzia, she's eighteen months old.

...Isn't it better to expect war than not to expect it?

...Having a child, all the more so. I have a presentiment of war.

...The thick layer of ice and the unregulated status of the Arctic meant that the race for deposits was delayed. After warming up, it became open to humankind, it's defenceless territory. The first Arctic war began on 21 April 2033, in the disputed Russian–Norwegian zone. Denmark declared itself on Russia's side, in the hope of extending its influence...

...All right, without the details, I'll just say that the result of the first war was Russia's military marginalization in the international arena, and as a consequence, in 2044, Greenland, being in fact a puppet state under the administration of US mining companies, declared independence. The US took command of the entire Arctic region, leaving its European part under the control of the Norwegians...

...And this? Oil paintings of the division of the world following the Arctic wars.

...The red one? That's the result of the Sinicization of the greater part of Russia. Here I've painted what resulted from all the Arctic wars. The title is *The Southern Hemisphere Following the Second Arctic War, 2047, Chinese People's Antarctica*. What's more, China will be the only indisputable superpower on Earth, ruler of the world. Here, these are my next pictures. This is *The Second Arctic War*, 2014, mixed technique, canvas, 90 x 90.

...If I keep on and on imagining the war like this I shouldn't be afraid of it, should I? In theory. After all, when you want to tell a person something painful, before saying it, you imagine your entire conversation. And once you've had that mental chat with yourself, you stop being scared of the conversation in reality. But I don't! I create war in my pictures, and yet I'm still terribly afraid of it.

...Here is a combination of an attack by Second World War troops and a nuclear explosion – all in one. Here I painted a city for my wife, which, I suspect, might not survive, because it'll be bombarded.

...Below there's a night patrol, and above there's a landscape after a battle.

...These are aircraft carriers on a red background amid black waves of crude oil, and this is the torpedo-launching platform at Babie Doły near Gdynia, near where they always hold the Open'er Festival. The Germans built it to carry out torpedo tests.

...But I won't agree. The torpedo-launching platforms will be used and we'll be witnesses of conventional war.

...Because only conventional war pays off. Financially. For all countries.

...'A Presentiment of War' – that's what I called my exhibition at the Pragaleria gallery in Warsaw. That's why the right-wing populist parties are winning worldwide, because people have a presentiment of war. Without this presentiment the political changes that we're seeing wouldn't be taking place.

...My family will survive.

...I'm a father, so it's a father's obligation to believe that his family will survive.

...*The Final Jump* – they're red people jumping from the sky with red parachutes ...

...I know they look like jellyfish, but they're parachutes.

...The fact that they haven't fallen to earth yet but they're not there anymore? Indeed, they're melting, but they haven't landed yet...

...Oh yes, that quote from Maria Janion is very apt: 'By living, we're losing life.'

...No. It's not we who'll jump, someone else will do it. It's never us, it's always someone else.

...They're pretty? That's because every war has its pleasant images, which appear later on. The TV series *Four Tankmen and a Dog*, for example, was a pleasant image of war years after it ended. Every war, especially in our country, becomes attractive after some time has passed. Maybe that's why people hunger for it later on. The young generation are particularly prone to that desire.

...A decorative war? There's something in that. Look at the frescoes and the old paintings. Eventually, war always becomes a decoration. War as decoration...

....Maybe 'said and painted by the artist Michał Mroczka'?

THE SOLDIER

He's come back from the war.

He spent a year and a half at the front.

He's sitting before an audience in a fairly large room. They have lots of questions, because it's rare for us to have someone from a war here.*

Is he talking too quietly into the microphone, or isn't it switched on? It is on – it's that he's talking too quietly.

He doesn't really want to say anything, and prefers to show photographs on a screen behind him. He shows 180 of them. 'Soldiers at war love to have their photo taken,' he says. 'They're extremely eager to pose. Why do they like it so much? I don't know,' he says.

The photos he has taken of the other soldiers at the front are excellent, because they're not nice. They're not trying to please. And they wouldn't be able to please anyone in Poland anyway. Soldiers sitting over a game of chess. Soldiers sitting on earth dug out of trenches, doing nothing. A soldier eating something from a metal bowl. Two of them sitting, that's all. 'And these

---

* The 'Pictures of War' event – Paweł Pieniążek in conversation with Mykhailo Kryven, a volunteer in the National Guard of Ukraine – took place on 4 July 2017 at the Wrzenie Świata bookshop in central Warsaw.

are selfies. They were all taken at a place called Krymske, ladies and gentlemen, near Luhansk.'

'Soldiers with computers. Playing games. What were they playing? A game called *Counter-Strike*, for instance, terrorists against anti-terrorists. And in *World of Tanks* you drive tanks on your mobile phone.'

'What's that? You play war games at a war?'

'At the front,' he explains, 'there's a short burst of fighting and then hours and hours of boredom. Two hours of shooting, for instance, and then what?'

The audience asks if in that case he can tell them about the war.

'Can you talk about Chopin's music with your fingers?' he says.

So there are the photos behind him. One of the soldiers has a card stuck on his backside that reads: 'PUTIN IS A DICKHEAD. LA LA LA LA.' 'That's a song we sang, to a very simple tune.'

The audience asks what the soldier's profession is.

A radiology engineer. His closest friends in the squad are a businessman, a teacher and a writer. They gave up their jobs and enlisted for the war.

The audience wants to know if it was worth engaging in armed conflict against the separatists.

'I don't know,' says the soldier.

'And is...?'

'I don't know... so I'll tell you something else – I was desperate for sweet things. We drank a lot of coffee, or rather, we didn't drink much coffee, because we only poured a drop of it into each mug, but then we added lots and lots of sweetened condensed milk. That was what everyone actually wanted, all of us. Before then, I'd never eaten sweets or cakes at home, but suddenly I couldn't live without them. I wonder why? I have no idea.'

The audience asks the radiology engineer: 'When you're at war, do you shoot to kill?'

'You shoot,' he explains. 'But you're glad the people you're firing at are firing too.'

'How come?' The audience doesn't understand.

'Because if they're firing at you it means they're alive and you haven't killed them... At the front, it was a problem that people's phones went on ringing – that was a real nuisance.'

'Yes, mobile phones ring at the front. For instance, my wife would call, from Ivano-Frankivsk. Once, in the middle of a dangerous bombardment, she called and asked: "There are no cheese forks." "What??" "Where are the cheese forks?" "I can't talk now, they're firing at us!" Anyway, my wife's here in the audience, she can tell the story herself.'

'It's true, I did make that call, a week after he left for the front. Because a friend came by, we made fondue, and you don't use ordinary forks for that. I couldn't find the special fondue forks anywhere. My husband hung up, so I started looking but I couldn't find them. Fifteen minutes later I rang him again, because he had to know where they were. He said he didn't.'

'Did she ever find them?' asks the audience.

'Yes. They were in a drawer.'

THE COLOURS HAVE RUN

I posted an advertisement on Facebook: 'I'm looking for people who are faking something, or pretending there's something missing from their life.'

The people who answered were all women, except for one.

The first woman to reply suffers from diabetes and Hashimoto's disease. Every day she pretends to be fit and well. Sometimes she can't tell anymore if her behaviour is the result of high blood sugar, or if it's just her character. A second woman writes that her life story consists of a series of events that happened to meet the needs of others. An ACA (adult child of alcoholics), she has discovered that 'all my life I've pretended to be go-ahead and happy, but I was and am nothing but an unappreciated child'. The third woman pretends that the young man she's been seen with lately is her boyfriend. She has a whole arsenal of replies ready to explain to her girlfriends why it hasn't worked out with him. And then a new imitation boyfriend appears. But in fact she's waiting for a woman to be in love with until the day she dies. A fourth one writes that she's been an expert at faking it for the past fifteen years: she pretends to be a happy mother. 'As time goes by, more and more often I come to the conclusion that I'm not suited to it, I don't want this burden, all these worries and cares. Why do people have to take tests to make sure they're fit to be drivers, but not to be parents?'

The fifth reply came from a man, aged thirty-six.

Karol has a shaven head, stubble, very nice teeth and a smile that's enough to make you forget that he's quite a small guy. He wears climbing boots, and in fact does a lot of hiking.

He works at a large department store. During breaks in the staff room, they talk about everything and anything, and the question 'What did you get as a first communion present?' comes up.

He thinks to himself: 'Karol was never baptized, so he didn't have a first communion.'

'Nothing, because I never took communion,' he replies, in keeping with the truth.

That way, he doesn't have to confess that, for first communion, he was given a pencil case with Alf on it.

Here, the copy editor of this book is sure to point out that you can confess to committing a crime, to having bad habits or to telling lies. But when it's about being given a pencil case, you could just 'not tell'.

And anyway, how come he never took communion, when he must have done, if he was given a pencil case?

First of all, Karol can't 'confess to' being given that pencil case for first communion.

Secondly, he never took first communion, though his parents would swear he did.

The breaktime conversations behind the scenes at the store are a challenge for Karol. A colleague starts to feel unwell, she feels hot, and she's laughing and crying by turns. So Karol asks if she's been to see a doctor. To which she says: 'My God, no bloke has ever asked me a question like that before.' The difference between what's actually going on in your head and what your hormones are prompting you to feel is something Karol knows very well. Lately, he has even started to consider divulging why he understands women so well. In his case, this understanding might not end well.

Karol says that when women fight for their rights, they latch on to a stereotype: they think he is bound to attack them, or at least be sceptical.

And then he has a moment of doubt: should he show support, or be sceptical? Or maybe be entirely against? What's his best bet?

Unfortunately, Karol lives according to his views: he goes to feminist demos, and when it comes to women's rights he's in favour of them.

I advise him to be careful, and not to express his opinions too hastily. Let's imagine that when a female colleague admits behind the scenes that she can't concentrate because she has her period he jumps up and says: 'I understand you perfectly!' The colleague stares at him with amazement. To which, also amazed by his own outburst, he says: 'When I was a busty blonde, I too had days when...' And the colleague then looks for a smile on his lips, which he only remembers to add after a few seconds' delay...

If Karol were to forget himself, he might confide in her that once upon a time, whenever he saw an ad for washing powder, it made him cry – he used to be upset at the mere sight of children getting their clothes dirty...

At college, he had a carefully thought-out way of talking about himself, and instead of 'I did all that studying and got a C,' he'd say: 'One does so much studying and gets a C.'

Using this grammatical form meant (more or less) that he could look himself in the eyes.

Karol took the offensive remark 'What sort of a homo is that?' aimed at him by youths on the tram as a compliment.

'I'm so pleased they got on here,' he'd think.

His granny had flashes of awareness in her dementia and mistook Karol for her deceased son.

'She couldn't have given me a greater gift,' he'd think.

I've just read this passage about Karol to a fellow reporter, Kamil Bałuk. 'Hold on a moment,' he said, 'this Karol fellow's a bit vague.' Yes, it's true. While I was reading it out to Kamil, I noticed the fogginess too. And it irritates me, as a reader. Who the hell is he? But I thought it was too early to introduce clarity. Karol's life has been going on a bit too long for me to freeze it in a couple of sentences according to the Hanna Krall school of reportage.

I've always wanted to find books left behind by someone who marked the quotes that mattered to them, and on that basis create a portrait of them.

Here are some of the passages that are underlined in Karol's books:

'All I really wanted was to try and live the life that was spontaneously welling up within me. Why was that so very difficult?' Hermann Hesse, *Demian*.*

'There was always a secret something in a person's house; something that shamed and thrilled them equally.' Jonathan Carroll, *White Apples*.

'To be nobody-but-yourself – in a world that's doing its best, night and day, to make you everybody else – means to fight the hardest battle which any human being can fight; and never stop fighting.' E.E. Cummings, *A Miscellany*.

'Men do change, and change comes like a little wind that ruffles the curtains at dawn, and it comes like the stealthy perfume of wildflowers hidden in the grass.' John Steinbeck, *Sweet Thursday*.

For Karol, this is a survival kit.

But why are all the authors of these thoughts men?

On 2 August 2008 Karol wrote under the sentence by Jonathan Carroll: 'I am the secret something in my own house. In my own family. Entire sentences remain unsaid, composed time and again out of doubt, fear and mutual resentment, the opposing imaginations of two generations. I was meant to be like them, but I'm not. I was meant to be easier and more predictable, but I'm not. I was meant to be nicer and cuddlier, but I'm

---

* Translated by Stanley Appelbaum.

not. More ha ha ha, hee hee hee. More convenient. I wasn't meant to be myself. But I am.'

It would have been all right if I'd ended it there. The reader would have had to work out the details that complete the sentence 'Karol pretends that in his life there's no...'. Or if I'd behaved like the American postmodernist Walter Abish. He'd get the readers going and then lead them to a fiasco, a lack of fulfilment. Must all works of reportage lay out the story flat on the floor and end it with a punch?

They must.

But why am I not serving up a linear story about Karol? Because the form should arise from the content, and Karol spent ages enduring the horror of his own lack of definition.

'And having no definition,' he explains, 'means being at odds with our own brains.'

'There are moments,' he adds, 'when I feel as if I've put my head in the washing machine, everything has gone spinning and the colours have run.'

We probably all enjoy a stroll through somebody else's life story. Without tripping over anything, without falling into any holes, but just gliding smoothly across the grass lawn of another person's life. I should have started this story with Karol's email, the fifth example in the gallery of replies to my advertisement on Facebook. Because in that email he showed his cards at once.

So let's glide along, here we go:

Mr Szczygieł, I was born and socialized as a little girl, a girl, a big girl, a woman. To the limits of my endurance.

I felt a strong bond with men, and I did my very best to demonstrate this in my appearance and behaviour – thus exposing myself to comments, attempts to get a rise out of me and belittlement, but I went ahead, purely and only because behaving like that made me feel coherent. I increasingly felt resentment at the fact that others were defining my needs.

Walls started to rise between me and them. 'Them' meaning boys. 'Them' meaning men. Those who had penises, when I did not. Those who loved girls.

They have, I haven't. They can, I can't.

I began twenty-seven years ago, when I stepped onto the path to transition. And today I'm on the other side of the mirror. I, Karol.

And you might think I no longer have to pretend, or mask anything, and now I'm an open book. But that's not the case.

My world has always been full of duality, and it's still with me. I'm aware of the complexities and ambiguities prevalent within it. My past is on the border of truth and concealment. Is that still 'hiding' or 'not fully revealing' myself?

I hide the sensitivity that has always been with me – the testosterone has failed to kill it. I hide myself in everyday life, in professional life, among people who don't know my transgender past. A former classmate who works for the same firm didn't realize I was Karolina. I hide what I'm feeling from others, what I know and how I perceive things.

On 8 March, when women come out into the streets with their demands, and I'm there with them, I'm quite often denied my right to my own feminism. Just because 'you're a bloke, you don't understand'. But in fact I'm on the other side of the barricade.

I know how much I earned and how I was treated as a woman, and how much I earn and am treated now. I can compare. I know!

I try my best to combine these two worlds within myself, because the first cannot exist without the second, and the second arises from the first.

With best wishes,
Karol.

When I ask why all the quotations are by male writers, Karol replies: 'I've always been on the masculine side of life!'

And that's coming from a man who goes to women's rights demos? Wow!

'For others to believe that I'm a man,' he replies, 'I had to spend years on end proving that I accept the things that define the stereotype of masculinity. And that I fit into that picture. But time has shown that I step outside many frames.'

(A little later, he adds: 'Am I a man if I like the colour pink?')

Going back to the lack of clarity in Karol's behaviour: he is long past menopause. He went through it between the twenty-fifth and the twenty-seventh year of his life. To remove his femininity, first it had to be extinguished. When his grandma mistook him for her son, Karol was pleased that she saw the man in him. When the youths on the tram shouted 'homo' he was pleased because they took him for gay, in other words saw him as a boy, rather than a girl.

We usually write to each other at night. I set Karol various tasks, and he's happy to perform them. I asked him to list what is not there in his life anymore.

'Breathlessness.'

'My surname with an -a ending.'*

'Poems. I stopped writing them thirteen years ago, shortly before my transition, and now nothing takes the form of poetry in my head. Prose, yes, but no poems anymore.'

'The hair on my head. I mourned for my hair. I had a dark-blonde bun...'

'A smooth face.'

'Singing. The timbre of my voice changed and a false note crept in, and now when I sing I'm out of tune.'

'My mammary glands and ovaries with their various appendages. I don't need them anymore. I never did.'

'Sensitive nipples.'

---

* Translator's note: many Polish surnames have grammatical endings that show gender. For instance, a man could be named Mr Kowalski, but a woman would be Ms Kowalska.

'Chest binders. They're used to disguise and flatten the breasts.'

'My school prom dress.'

'The TV set.'

'A poster for the movie *Rocky* with the quote "His whole life was a million-to-one shot", which used to warm me up for the fight.'

'Boring, colourless socks. Before my transition I promised myself they'd be more colourful afterwards. I dreamed of having colours in my life.'

'Depression.'

'Lack of confidence and doubts. Who am I, how am I to help myself, can I cope?'

'The feeling that I'm stuck in a waiting room.'

'Kasia Kowalska tapes and mangling the song "Pain".'

'Clutter. I discovered the salutary effect of minimalism on my life spontaneously, by realizing that I'd rather be than have. Which doesn't preclude the fact that I'm a bit of a gadget geek.'

'Frequent walks around the cemetery. The thought of death had a calming effect on me.'

'Taboo topics.'

'Fear of having a conversation.'

'Karolina is not there. I went through a sort of grieving process for her, I worked it through in therapy.'

'Crying during advertising breaks (it was my hormones crying, not me).'

'The fear of being caught out. As if I constantly had to hide my own truth from someone.'

'My anxieties: that I couldn't manage, that I'd be lonely, that no one would want me, that I was inadequate, incomplete, too weak, that I didn't deserve it.'

'God.'

'A sense of guilt.'

'Shame.'

'The thought of being in suspension, the feeling that "I don't know from where, to where, for what". As if that "for what" was at all necessary.'

'Hope of love. I swapped it for working on having some love for myself and accepting reality. Without any expectations.'

What is definitely there in his life?

'A penis.'

The decided majority of men want their penis to be of use. It's the centre of their micro-universe. The more interest the world shows in their penis, the greater their self-satisfaction.

'Karol, has anyone ever wanted to see your penis?'

'That's a prickly issue,' he wrote back. 'Believe it or not, nobody has wanted to see it. Including people who know I was Karolina and am now Karol, and people who don't know.'

(That was going to be my culminating point.

This sort of story doesn't only tell you about the person at the centre of it, but also contains a hidden subtext about the author. You might wonder whether choosing these episodes, and not others, from the subject's life doesn't say more about the person writing than the person being written about. I decided to end with the penis. I wanted to show that, thanks to it, Karol has something, but that at the same time there's something missing.

It's very likely that the penis matters to me.

When Karol read this piece about himself, he replied:

'Your text is sinking in while I'm on my way to the mountains. That ending – what an irony! The penis – as the ending, the penis – as the climax! Like a pebble in your shoe. I promised myself I wouldn't interfere in your story, in the way you perceive, filter and recreate me. With one exception – if something doesn't tally with the truth/the facts. So let's go back to the prickly issue.

'If I had to answer the question "What *is there*?" I'd say: "A sense of being adequate."

'For others perhaps the penis is a road sign, an indicator, and I've taken away its decision-making power. I'm still learning how to be a guy with no balls, maybe sometimes in ballsing around with it there's more of an irreverent approach in me than solemnity.

'If the meaningful point is to be that my life revolves around my penis or that my penis sets the pace for me, that's not the case. My penis can go hang!')

A NUMBER OF MANLY SCENES

SCENE 1

Three men go up to a car.

'Who's getting in the back with him?' asks the Driver.

He opens the rear door: a figure with its knees tucked up to its chin, bundled in bubble wrap and girded with sticky tape, is lying on the seat. A pair of bare feet protrudes from the plastic.

'Jeezus Christ! I've got bad associations since the murder of that Polish lorry driver in Berlin,' says the one who was about to get in the back.

'Hop in,' says the Driver. 'I'll shift him up a bit. It won't take us long to get there, about ten minutes, you'll survive.'

SCENE 2

From a recording made in the car, in Warsaw city centre:

Passenger 1 to Passenger 2: 'Is he moving?'

Passenger 2: 'Noooo.'

Driver: 'First we'll park the car near the philharmonic. We'll get out without him and survey the terrain. When you drive from Złota Street into the tunnel under Marszałkowska Avenue there's a sort of skylight in the tunnel. First of all, let's go and take a look. We won't drive into it straight away. I'll show you the spot from above, we'll go back to the car quietly, and only then head into the tunnel.'

Passenger 1: 'How do we get him out without anyone noticing?'

Driver to Passenger 1: 'There's one method that works for me. I stop the car, set up the triangle, fetch out the spare wheel and a child seat...'

Passenger 1: 'We haven't got a child.'

Driver: 'We don't need one. The seat and the triangle supply positive information. But we don't want any drivers stopping to help. So you'll stand there with your phone and pretend to be talking to someone.'

Passenger 1: 'OK.'

Driver: 'Then it looks as if you've called for help on your mobile. That means you're dealing with it, and no one will stick their oar in. But while you're talking on the phone you must keep looking in both directions to watch out for the city guard or the police.'

Passenger 1: 'Great!'

Driver: 'I'll open the door on the side next to the wall and pull him out.'

Passenger 2: 'Can you do it on your own?'

Driver: 'I managed to get him into the car by myself! He's not heavy. He weighs less than you or I. He's of slight build.'

SCENE 3

They're standing above the tunnel. The Driver points out the spot where the tiled wall is bisected by a slanting shadow. On the bright part of the wall it's a sunny morning, surprisingly, for two days before Christmas Eve, and on the dark part it's the evening, lit by streetlamps.

'He has to end up on the border of the shadow,' says the Driver and looks down. 'Because only then does it make sense.'

SCENE 4

The car stops in the tunnel. The rear door opens on the side facing the wall to shield the Driver, who places a template with three holes in it on the narrow pavement. He puts on a pair of gloves and uses a hammer drill to make holes in the paving blocks. They won't be disturbed by anyone on foot, because pedestrians are not allowed in the tunnel. The noise of the drill is swallowed by the din of traffic on the road.

I am no longer Passenger 1, but Man Holding a Phone to His Ear.

Passenger 2 is the Photographer, and he goes off to take pictures of the operation from various perspectives.

The Driver is Father of the Huddled Figure, who is still lying on the rear seat swathed in plastic.

Unfortunately our car takes up half the lane, so the other drivers are slowing down to pass us. Luckily, the city guard vehicle comes the other way, so it doesn't slow down. The Huddled Figure, thank God, goes on lying there and can't be seen.

The Father of the Huddled Figure quickly squirts silicone into the holes he has drilled, pulls the curled-up character out through the rear door, positions him on the template so it's easier to put in the screws, tightens them and tears off the plastic. Without waiting for the Photographer, we get in the car and drive off towards the Palace of Culture.

The Huddled Figure is left all alone with the city.

We drive around the streets and three minutes later we drive back into the tunnel again. To see how he looks at his post, with those sad, goggling eyes.

So there on the edge of the shadow sits a squatting figure, looking straight at those driving in. It can also be seen from above, through the skylight, as you walk along Marszałkowska Avenue between the Centrum shopping mall buildings. Our Driver slows down, and at last I can take a look: the Huddled Figure is naked, his arms are embracing his knees, and the fingers of his right hand seem to be digging into the left. The artist has marked his entire body with streaks of rain: they're flowing from under his fingers, they're flowing down his back, and two separate ones are flowing from his eyes.

He looks as if it were his task to give Warsaw sorrow.

'He looks as miserable as fuck,' confirms the Driver, with satisfaction.

AN EXPLANATION

It's time to drop the word 'Driver', because that was just Tomasz Górnicki's supporting role, alongside Tomasz Górnicki the sculptor.

My admiration for him stems from the fact that I think the way he behaves is exactly how a man should behave.

And that's my reason for writing this text.

JESUS NUMBER ONE

A man – in this case Tomasz Górnicki, born in 1986, married to Ewa, father of Kosma (aged 4) and Tytus (aged 4 months); graduate of the Sculpture Faculty of the Academy of Fine Arts in Warsaw, where he studied under Professor Antoni Janusz Pastwa – knows how to assign a new task to Jesus.

In Częstochowa, for instance, he got him to disappear and then reappear. I have never assigned a task to Jesus, so I asked Górnicki for the details.

'In Blessed Virgin Mary Avenue there are some kebab stalls,' he said. 'And that's where my Christ appeared, having come down from his cross.'

Jesus is sitting down on a steel pedestal, holding a cigarette, and there's a rusty cross behind him.

'What's he got there? Is he naked?' I asked, as I stared at the picture.

'He just has flip-flops on his feet.'

'And what's that written on them?'

'"Kubota".'

(Chinese Kubota flip-flops are famous in Poland. Polish men have two aesthetic obsessions: grey-brown clothes and Kubota flip-flops. If you see a guy hurrying to the off-licence in dirty white socks and flip-flops, with his toes sticking out of them at the front, you can bet your bottom dollar they're Kubota flip-flops. For eight zlotys a pair they'll strip anyone of their sex appeal.)

'The question arises,' continues the artist, 'whether Christ has come down from his cross after two thousand years of hanging there because he can't bear to go on looking at what's happening, and has been for a kebab in Częstochowa, or whether it's just another fancy-dress freak in those flip-flops and you can take your picture with him. Where the abbreviation INRI usually appears on the cross I've put the message "GIVE ME A BREAK", which is also the title of the work as a whole. Colloquially rather than literally, with the right intonation, that phrase means "For God's sake! What the...!" We put him on display on the day a pilgrimage from Warsaw reached the Jasna Góra Monastery,* when some ten thousand people were walking down the avenue. But the people didn't believe in him – they kept carrying him off into the bushes. My pals came

---

* Translator's note: the Jasna Góra Monastery in the city of Częstochowa is home to the Black Madonna, Poland's most sacred icon, and is the destination for devout pilgrims who come great distances on foot (or, traditionally, on their knees).

at night to look for the poor fellow in the undergrowth and set him up again, either on a low wall, or near a stall, or in the middle of the avenue. And I stress: he was never destroyed. As Jesus, he may have hurt their feelings, but he was still Jesus!'

'And where is he now?'

'No one knows, because about a month later he disappeared for good.'

This is the first time I've ever heard of sending a sculpture into the unknown.

THEFT, OR IN OTHER WORDS A DIALOGUE

A man also knows how to decide where Jesus is to do his blessing. He decided that the right place was on the East–West Route in Warsaw, a major road that crosses the city, partly underground.

When you drive into the tunnel that takes the road under the grand city-centre street named Krakowskie Przedmieście, there are niches in the walls. These niches, Tomasz says, are just asking for something to be displayed in them. So in one of them he placed the hands of Jesus in a gesture of benediction. In the next niche, for company, he placed the hands of the Virgin Mary in her open-armed pose. The first work is called *You're Going on Alone*, and the second is *Mother, Where Are Your Children?* Pedestrians can't go in there, and the cars drive fast, so there was little chance of the hands performing any function. But a radio reporter found her way to the niches, photographed them and then showed the pictures to the people waiting at the nearest bus stop. Which, admittedly, is a rather weird occurrence – thanks to someone the artist didn't know, his sculpture finally reached its audience, but in the form of a photograph.

The audience at the bus stop immediately understood what the hands were trying to say. (The sculptor heard this later, on the radio.)

'If you tear through here on a motorbike, those hands seem to be shouting: "Stop! Slow down!",' said a young man.

'Well yes, the East–West Route tunnel was dug out of the ruins of post-war Warsaw, so those are the hundreds of victims who were never extracted, and now they're coming out of the walls,' said an old woman.

The sculptor says he was impressed by this simple human message.

The hands stayed fixed to the wall for a month. Where they are protruding from now is not known. If someone has stolen Mary's and Jesus' hands, that's great. Tomasz Górnicki told me the name he gives to theft: 'dialogue'.

'I like that sort of public dialogue,' he added.

JESUS UNDER THE BRIDGE

A man, if needs be, is able to find a safe refuge for Jesus. He hung Christ up in a sheltered spot under a railway bridge in Warsaw's Solec district, where hardly anyone can see him. Which makes a lot of sense.

He can only be seen by those who chance to stop under the bridge's span – at the point where it's darkest, so not many do stop – and look up. At a height of four metres, in a nook onto which a streak of light falls from above, hangs the naked figure of a man. And in almost a year, no one has removed it. This must be a Jesus with a strong will to survive.

'But he hasn't got a cross,' I remarked.

'My friend, the painter and architect Daniel Chazme, made some flat rusting blocks out of steel,' explained Tomasz. 'We fixed them to the stone wall and hung him on this abstract composition. It was about the tonal transition from the existing world into the world of art. He may not have Jesus' props, but as soon as you glance at him you have a sense of the figure ascending. The narrow space and the light create the impression of a chapel.'

'But Tomasz, he hasn't got a loincloth! Jesus doesn't hang around in church with his penis on parade. What's more, his is a bit too big, as far as I can tell. Who was the model?' I was curious to know.

'It was me,' replied the sculptor. 'I didn't want him to be suffering, I wanted him to be an attractive young man. I associate the church with suppressed sexual energy. The grannies engrossed in prayer for whom sex is just a memory have singled out this young man for themselves. They often kiss him on the feet, they adore him. So there they have a dear little naked Jesus, ascending to heaven.'

(They no longer have him. A year later, Jesus – whose will to survive was not as strong as I'd thought – turned to rubble.

Someone climbed up the wall and threw him off it. A man working in an office near the bridge found Jesus' remains at a bus stop, with a dog-end placed in his hand.)

ONE QUESTION

It's clear that a man is not going to ask anyone for permission for what he does. He leaves his mark on the city wherever he wishes. He shoves whatever he likes into its nooks and crannies.

ETIQUETTE

Of course, the sculptor won't say it's about being a man. He calls it urban intervention, or, more interestingly, guerrilla sculpture.

An art expert would count this activity as street art, although that is mainly associated with pictures spray-painted on the walls of buildings. So perhaps they would label it more broadly as urban art.

He has had exhibitions. But exhibiting in a gallery is like the gene pool of the Finns. Isolation meant that, for whole centuries, the genes of the Finns were not replaced, and as a result many of the Finns' organisms began to attack themselves with strange illnesses. The same twenty or thirty people keep coming to Tomasz's private views, and over time he has come to know them all. It's mainly students and professors from the academy who turn up, so it's hard for them to surprise each other.

But standing under a bridge craning your neck and staring up at Christ is quite different from looking at him in a gallery. What's more, I suspect that a sculpture stands in a gallery for applause. It's waiting to be stroked, it says nothing.

Outside the gallery it talks away and says what the hell it likes.

I'M GOING BACK TO JESUS

But only briefly, to avoid overdoing the religious theme.

Tomasz comments in an email: 'Can you imagine a man in agony in an electric chair hanging above the door in people's houses? Or children getting a little gold electric chair as a pendant for first communion? Jesus on the cross is a horrific image, but no one's shocked by that violence. Yet another Jesus on the cross is just a copy of the same old thing that no one stops to think about. It's the trivialization of suffering. Nothing sells better than sex and violence – maybe that explains the success of the Christian religion? The most basic stimulants dressed in golden robes.'

Once, I said, 'You keep going back to God.'

'That's because I'm a non-believer,' he explained. 'We call him to account more often because we have more questions. The believers don't have to ask questions, because they have ready answers. And look,' he added, 'however much I disown this God fellow, he keeps working away in me!'

When a man hears a view he disagrees with, he corrects it.

Take the Japanese proverb about the three wise monkeys. The Japanese have carved and painted them for centuries: one monkey is covering its eyes, so it sees no evil. The second is covering its ears and hears no evil. The third is covering its mouth and speaks no evil. As if someone deaf and blind to evil is meant to protect themselves from it.

Tomasz Górnicki takes a dim view of this idea, because turning away from evil is evil. And so at exactly twelve noon on 1 January 2016 he intervened. On a wall in the passage between Constitution Square and Koszykowa Street in central Warsaw, he mounted the heads of three fat men of Asian appearance. One had sticking-out ears for hearing, another had goggling eyes for seeing, and the third had his mouth wide open. On the side of their skulls were the words 'HEAR', 'SEE', 'SHOUT'.

Tomasz regarded it as a New Year's resolution.

It turns out that not only the form and the content are essential to a work of art, but also the date and the hour.

In the photos – which is all we have left, because the public dialogue with the heads began the very next day – you can see that the author has mounted them on a stained, decaying wall. Tomasz has no desire to sully the unsullied. Fresh walls, renovated sites and manicured corners don't interest him. As someone who works with his hands he knows that a labourer who has plastered or painted a wall has put an effort into it.

He respects the work of others. He also checks the register of listed buildings. If a building is of historical importance, he leaves it alone.

HOW TO HOODWINK

A man has to have some frontline camouflage techniques:

'When we'd just finished installing *Hear, See, Shout*, a guy suddenly appeared and demanded explanations. So of course I boldly said: "I've been in touch with the administration." "With whom?" "With Marek." "Which Marek?" "I have no idea. I spoke to Marek, who gave us permission to drill here. But who *he's* in touch with I have no idea." "Then I'll check." "No problem." But it was the first of January, so I doubted he had a way to check. Off he went, and I said: "OK, boys, we're out of here!" And on the East–West Route there's a complete ban on pedestrians entering the tunnel, and the police caught me twice while I was putting up the hands. But each time I brazenly lied my way out of it, saying I was doing a job for the Modern Art Foundation, a project financed by the European Union. I wouldn't let them get a word in. "But where's your permit?" "I have no idea, please ask the curator of the exhibition." Policeman: "No, when you bring a permit, you can carry on." And I say: "All right, all right." The more brazen you are, the better it works. I waited for them to leave, and went back to the attack with my drill. Because Mary's and Jesus's hands were set into the walls on screws that long.' (He shows their length.)

Hoodwinking others is Tomasz's speciality.

The London-based artist Ben Eine, whose chunky letters appeared on walls and became legendary, was famous for his camouflage skills. When he was still a graffiti artist, rather than a designer for Louis Vuitton, he specialized in misleading the guards. In those days he was working for an insurance firm. He'd go out in his office clothes, in other words a suit and tie, and set about the walls dressed like that. Whenever the police turned up, he'd hide the tin of paint and start to read a newspaper.

A MAN AND HIS FRIENDS

A man knows how to get even with the friends who've let him down.

The skulls are standing on pedestals and hanging on walls. The large shed near the Górnickis' house is full of skulls. Some are rusty, some have holes in them, others are polished, shiny, matt, coloured, white, black, cubist, organic, made of rags, hard, soft, dirty, clean, patterned, suffering, peaceful, shouting, silent, with teeth, without teeth, with eyes and without eyes. And one (not nice) is studded with nails like in voodoo.

'I'll give you the short version,' said Tomasz, opening the topic of the skulls. 'I moved out of Warsaw to live here in the countryside because I was rejected by a group of friends. The reason for the conflict is not for public display. I cut off all ties with them. But unless you go to a psychotherapist, you have to find a way to deal with that sort of thing. So I made nine skulls.'

He must have noticed my surprise, because he added: 'Each one belongs to one of them.'

His wife Ewa was strolling among the pedestals with little Tytus in her arms. She was showing the baby how the setting sun was reflected in a golden skull. She would soon go off to the Pilates class she runs for local enthusiasts. At the Jagiellonian University, she wrote a paper on the sacred and the profane in capoeira. She and Tomasz met thanks to this martial art; she was nineteen and he was fifteen. And so the classic idea concerning capoeira – that anyone who practises it discovers the truth – came true.

Ewa turned away from the golden skull and inspected how Tomasz was standing.

He works hard physically, and she makes sure that he's conscious of how he's standing, bending over and kneeling down, because he has to remain fit and well. Tomasz took Tytus in his arms and showed me the conscious way he holds a baby, then his wife took the child back and went off.

'Despite the rift, we invited two of them to our wedding,' he said, returning to the subject of his friends. 'The one who's a notorious singleton suddenly said to me: "You know what, a wife's a wife, but as Leszek Kołakowski always said the most important people in life are your friends…" At my wedding! It's a wonder I didn't hang him on the fence. "Leszek Kołakowski was a great man," I said, "but the most important people are your family." It's herd philosophy to think that our boys' gang is what matters, and a female is just an extra. A female isn't just an extra. Or just a female.'

'But Tomasz,' I said, dismayed, 'you've got at least a hundred of these skulls! Where do they all come from?'

'Do you know the Nirvana song "Lithium"?' he asked. 'The one where he says he's happy today because he found his friends – they're in his head.'

The way I understood this is that his best friends are now the ones he invents for himself. And the whole place is full of their skulls.

SCULPTING A BOOK

A man reads a book and decides to carve its content in stone. The book is *Like Eating A Stone* by Wojciech Tochman, about the war in Bosnia.

We were standing in a field, with the woods ahead of us and the big shed behind us, as well as Ewa and Tomasz's house, and a bit further off the village, which isn't visible from there. On the frozen ground there was a hospital bed with a mattress and a crumpled sheet made of granite.

'You could say that is Tochman's bed,' Tomasz informed me.

'How do you mean?'

'The title of the book came from the story of a woman whose husband was killed by the Serbs. Remember? And that husband appears to her at night, but says nothing. He doesn't even ask about their child. He just stares and knows everything. And when she wakes up, her son tells her she was grinding her teeth again, as if she were eating a stone.'

'That's a passage that affects my nervous system,' I said.

'Mine too,' he agreed.

'I read it to my students each year, because I use Tochman to teach that less is more.'

'As in sculpture. I used to teach it using Rodin, though I'm not a fan, and Bałka, whose work I like. So I read Tochman, and then I started grinding my teeth too, until my jaw and head began to ache, so I spent two weeks going from doctor to doctor. Finally one of them said it was to do with my nerves.'

'Not a lack of magnesium?'

'Nervous lockjaw. I ground my teeth so hard I thought my head would explode. And it was also connected with the story of my family. And one night that stone sheet occurred to me. Often, when I read a book, I try to visualize my impressions. I think about how to dress its content in my language. Anyone who lies on that bed has a very nasty experience. I know, because I've lain and sat on it naked. The mattress weighs three hundred kilos. Plenty of work for the grinding machine. A lot of blood, sweat and tears went into making it look wrinkled. But that's not an ordinary bed from a hospital storeroom, it was welded together from scratch and then aged by me. I also have work that references Tochman's book about Rwanda, *Today We're Going to Draw Death*.'

'That's a dangerous book. You can lose your faith in humanity from reading it,' I said.

'Yes, but when I hold my best living four-kilo sculpture in my arms and he smiles at me, or when my other stupendous four-year-old sculpture comes and chats with me, I recover my faith immediately. Or when Ewa and I lull both sculptures to sleep. And that's as complicated a process as launching Apollo 13...'

'I'M SORRY' ISN'T ENOUGH

'Ewa and I were on holiday at the seaside, and we did some people-watching,' says Tomasz.

'At the Polish seaside,' I specify.

'Yes. We saw how at every step of the way parents instil a sense of guilt in their children. It's striking. "We would have gone, but because of you..." "You see, you always have to..." "You're not getting any ice cream because you..." The children do something wrong, or do nothing, and at once the parent is scoring off them. The belief that they're doing something wrong is constantly beaten into the child.'

'"Tua culpa",' I specify.

'I remember going to church as a small boy and beating my chest – mea culpa, mea culpa... What culpa, for fuck's sake? Why on earth beat a sense of guilt into a person from when they're little?'

'To have control over them. It's about power,' I specify.

'Lots of children repeat it automatically in church. But what if that sense of guilt continues into their adult life? So I came home from the seaside and started to take action with both barrels... Under a bridge, near the Stradom Station in Częstochowa, I put a little boy. He was naked, kneeling on the gravel with his head drooping. His hands were tied behind his back with wire. I wanted his head to be at the height of an adult's thigh – I wanted to see if anyone noticed him and approached him to try and help, for instance. He was kneeling between some concrete pillars, and the bridge acted like a roof, as if shielding him, but at the same time oppressing, crushing him. His legs were sunk into the ground...'

'And that was your older son, Kosma,' I specify.

'Yes. Because I'd never seen an image like it anywhere, so I had to have a prototype.'

'But he didn't pose for his father with his hands tied,' I specify.

'No. I tried not to involve him in that project. It's a tough piece: when the boy was standing, or rather kneeling, under that bridge, it looked even more powerful. My son knows they're not real people. He has seen himself in various sculptures of mine and he knows his father made it. He's able to separate art from life.'

'He knows it's plaster,' I specify.

'Yes, twenty-five kilos. The title of the work is *"I'm Sorry" Isn't Enough*. I used to hear those words as a child. You know my dad, he's a volcano of energy and he's quite explosive too. I once did something wrong as an eleven-year-old, and I apologized to him. "You can shove your apology up your arse," he said. Since then, I have never said "I'm sorry" to him again. When I've got up to mischief I've admitted my guilt, but not said "I'm sorry".'

'You didn't want your words shoved up your arse again,' I specify.

'Things rankle with me, I've got the memory of an elephant. It's easy to crush a young person. When you have power you should be careful not to abuse it. I say sorry to my son. I come in at night and say sorry to him.'

'But for now he's the one saying sorry. As a sculpture,' I specify.

'I think it's me. I sculpted myself. I regard it as a self-portrait. But not only that, because one is at the same time victim and oppressor. You give what you get. Unless you put a stop to it yourself. My father was harsh towards me, so I try to be milder. But do I succeed? Childhood is not a time when you should be afraid of your parents!'

'And I'm recording that as the truth of this section,' I specify.

'You're familiar with my sculptures and you know they decay or get stolen from the places where I install them, but something worse happened to this boy. I made a special effort to protect that sculpture. I dug a pit, set a concrete block in it, attached the boy to the block with wires, and poured the plaster. But someone destroyed him – they didn't just tip him over, tear him out and take him away. They battered him to pieces. With an iron bar? Or a brick perhaps? The entire body was smashed to smithereens. The head had been ripped off. Someone had gone completely apeshit. You'd have to try really hard to break it to bits like that. And what on earth was that person thinking? I offer up a sculpture about aggression, and it meets with aggression. Couldn't he bear the subject of that image? Trauma or stupidity? And if he's stupid enough to fuck up a sculpture, maybe he's also stupid enough to...'

'...beat up his child or his wife,' I finish the sentence.

LEAVING YOUR MARK ON THE WORLD

When a man goes on holiday, he must leave his mark too.

Tomasz Górnicki went to Greece with his family, and he also took a stone chisel. On Crete, at the village of Psari Forada, he asked his wife – so he says – to give him thirty-five minutes to himself, and ran to the rock sticking out furthest towards Africa. And he carved a pair of lips on it. A woman's lips. They're closed, they're not saying anything. When Professor Pastwa saw them he said they contain a promise.

When he went to Iceland, he took some small golden twigs. Real twigs from Mazovian trees, which he cast in bronze and gilded at a jeweller's. He planted them outside Reykjavik in a volcanic rock full of holes. He called them lost thoughts.

MY MANLINESS

As you can see, Tomas Górnicki's manliness is dynamic and impressive. Whereas mine manifests itself, at most, on walks.

I take evening strolls for the good of my alcohol-fattened liver. Strenuous walking helps the fat surrounding it to break down into carbon dioxide and water. The former I exhale, and the latter I sweat and pee out.

But breath, sweat and urine are not much for a man to offer the world. So I'd like to be a sculptor in my next incarnation, please.

LUNCH EN FAMILLE

'We drink alcohol, we like alcohol. Our family drinks a thousand bottles of wine a year,' declared Tomasz's father at the table. 'But thank God or whatever we've never become alcoholics. What's more,' he added – Waldemar Górnicki specializes in having the final word – 'there's nothing better than pulling your socks up, having a meal with your family, having a drink with your family and rising from the table with your head reeling. Well, let's say the only thing that's better is work.'

Because after installing the Huddled Figure the three of us went for lunch at the village outside Warka where all the Górnickis live in two neighbouring properties. We planned to return to Warsaw a few hours later, after dusk, to see how the lights of the city made the Huddled Figure's eyes glitter. And for the Photographer to take some nocturnal pictures of him. Norbert Piwowarczyk's photos are part of every project, and later the only evidence that's left of them.

On the way I finally found out how Tomasz earns a living. All the manoeuvres described above are the result of a compulsion for which he must cover the cost. He told us about a wealthy client who wants to have himself sculpted in bronze, life-size, but for some reason with very large private parts.

'It's to have the balls of a bull,' said Tomasz, giving us the precise details, because that was how the customer put it.

We toured both the parents' and the children's houses. We walked across an impressive space, where sculptures stand under the open sky. We went into the foundry. This is where the father works; he also left Warsaw and gave up his job in business. Now he casts the work of sculptors from all over the world. In a building Waldemar has put up for himself and for his son, Tomasz has his workshop too. There in the dust, among tools, machinery and human body parts, I saw a picture of the music critic Bogusław Kaczyński.

'I know that face like the back of my hand,' explained Tomasz. 'I've stared at it for hours.'

'And what is there to see in it?'

'Symmetry and heartache.'

He also makes his living from this sort of commission. He has already prepared Bogusław Kaczyński's gravestone. He has started to sculpt his head eleven times but never finished. All because the world is extremely unfair – so said Bogusław Kaczyński, and having read that remark, Tomasz wants to reflect it in the sculpted face.

We sat down to lunch with his parents. Their house and everything inside it is on a grand scale. If the kitchen is vast, the sitting room is gigantic. The locals can't believe it's a building for living in. Mama, who with her platinum buzz cut would look quite at home in a music video, announced goose. She cooks every day, sometimes making as many as three soups, all different. Before moving to the countryside, she was a psychotherapist in Warsaw. But here she has come to believe that anyone who's not in a life-threatening situation should draw on their own physical resources. She doesn't want to hear patients saying 'I've no one except you' anymore. She'd rather hear it from her family. Górnicki Senior emerged from the sauna in a dressing gown, tall, burly and smiling. He announced that he'd get dressed and serve the wine in a jiffy.

And now I could see where Tomasz gets his courage, big-heartedness and lack of inhibitions. Because his father, a man of fifty-six at the time of our meeting, whose photographic nudes I'd seen in various parts of the house, then uttered a courageous remark. A disinterested remark. A remark that would never emerge from the lips of a typical Polish man. And if it did, that man would instantly punch himself in the face for saying it.

'Mr Szczygieł,' he said, 'once in a while men should go into the sauna together and touch todgers. I recommend it.'

AVIDITY

Once Waldemar and I had moved on to first-name terms, I asked him to explain the family's temperament and tendency to take risks.

Waldemar's reply: Dalmatia.

In the late nineteenth century, when Bosnia came under Habsburg rule, the poorest people from Galicia were encouraged to leave. So his great-grandfather was given a mountain in the vicinity of a village named Dubrava Stara. When the Habsburg empire collapsed, the Poles became citizens of a new state: the Kingdom of Serbs, Croats and Slovenes. In 1946 the Polish People's Republic encouraged them to return to the Recovered Territories, and that was how they ended up in Bolesławiec. Tomasz's father was born there. Except that his grandfather, who was a roisterer, had sold the entire Balkan property and drunk the money away before returning to Poland. Anna, Tomasz's mum, says that those who had the risk-taking gene boarded the train to Poland. The others stayed behind and died of starvation.

Waldemar claimed that all this is exactly why Tomasz has such an avidity for life.

'When the war in the Balkans ended, my dad said I should go and find out if his cousin was still alive,' Waldemar began. 'It was 1996, I fetched Tomek, and off we went. When we reached the village, I looked around and saw three old boys drinking rakia from a sort of canister with a tap. One of them turned round, I looked again, and saw the face of my father! And in the voice of my father, he asked where we were from... To this day, I distil rakia the Serbian way.'

'Dad, tell him something more serious,' asked Tomasz.

'About Reza,' added Anna.

'Reza spent seven years in the cellar. My cousin kept his Muslim wife in the cellar so they wouldn't kill her. Who? The neighbours. And when we arrived she came out of the cellar, but she couldn't speak anymore.'

SCENE 5

The three men go back to the city centre. In an animated tone, the Driver explains that he understands the edge of the shadow from three perspectives: 1) that of the spectator/crowd viewing the work; 2) that of the figure, as someone who has ended up in the shadow and is suffering; from that angle it is looking at the passers-by; 3) that of the figure, as someone who consciously chooses to sit in shadow, which is their refuge. Passenger 1 wonders if he's capable of writing that out as a lively, vibrant conversation.

They drive into the tunnel. Close-up: the corners of their mouths rapidly turn from up to down. The view from the car window: the Huddled Figure is not there. There are just three empty holes on the paving blocks.

'Oh my God,' says Passenger 2.

'Oh fuck!' exclaims the Driver. 'That's a record! The shortest surviving sculpture ever...'

'Six hours and it's not there?' says Passenger 1, amazed.

'It's not there! And I really wanted to have a photo of the glint in his eye at night,' says the Driver, sounding disappointed. 'Up there, people are running from shop to shop looking for presents, while he squats down here, hidden, chilled to the bone, waiting for Christmas. Like an urban pigeon. Homeless, a runaway, maybe a refugee.'

They come to the conclusion that in all probability he was taken away by the city services; the three of them had forgotten that everything they did on the edge of the shadow at noon was being watched by two panoramic cameras on two of the shopping centre buildings.

Close-up: the Driver's eyes are even sadder than those of the Huddled Figure.

The cat was brought to him by his closest friend. He'd found it in the park. The animal had followed his bike. Whenever he stopped cycling, the cat had sat down, and even lain down beside his bike.

The cat was just as friendly to its new master as it had been to the cyclist: on the first night in its new home, it lay down on the owner's belly.

The cat, who was in fact a she-cat, was given the name Holka, which is the Czech word for 'girl'. It soon became apparent that the cat was female, because she was pregnant. Two months later, in a box lined with a towel and placed behind the wardrobe in the bedroom, Holka gave birth to three sons. Each had two of her four colours. One son was white and beige, another was black and white, and the third was grey and black. In the morning when her master opened the bedroom door (she had spent the night on her own in there), Holka had already licked the kittens clean. At the sight of her master she meowed loudly, as if she thought it appropriate to say something. Perhaps she was reporting 'mission accomplished'?

That afternoon, she left the kittens and lay down on his belly. After a while she remembered her children and ran to the box behind the wardrobe. It occurred to him that she was just a child who needed lots of petting, but also had children of her own now.

Two months later, Holka's sons found new homes. It did them good, because she had stopped paying attention to them a while ago. She only took notice of her master. He would turn her onto her back, lean over her belly and breathe in the scent of her fur. He could cuddle her, spar with her, and even drape her around his neck. She liked jumping on the heads of people with long hair without warning. She couldn't let her intentions show, because as soon as she craned her neck towards them, the object of her attention would move away – it was obvious she was about to leap at them. So she found a way to leap up unexpectedly, with a vertical take-off. She could jump onto someone's shoulder in a straight line, from under their feet. Then the long-haired people would seat her on their necks themselves, and she'd rub her head against their hair. Her master's friends were convinced the cat had run away from a circus, and even called her 'the acrobat cat'.

Whenever the master came home, he said to her: 'Hello, my darling little bundle of joy.'

You don't do that to a human being.

In the twelfth year of their life together, the master started to feel tiny lumps under the cat's skin. The specialists said they were caused by a pancreatic tumour. The close friend who had brought the cat over twelve years ago because she had sat and even lain down beside his bicycle began to stay with her during the day when her master was out at work. The cat would climb onto the bottom shelf in the wardrobe and lie there on the underwear. 'She stays there for hours on end,' the friend told her master.

'And what do you do?'

'I lie on the rug by the open wardrobe door, but she doesn't react to anything. Though I do talk to her. Sometimes I sing to her.'

They went to the vet's together. 'I can give her an injection that will get her through the weekend,' said the vet, 'but it'd be pure selfishness.'

Neither man wanted to be selfish.

It was early February 2012, and the weather was very cold. They wondered how they'd manage to dig a hole in the ground. The vet reassured them that the clinic had an incinerator, and the cat would be cremated according to their usual procedures.

The close friend was desperately upset as they said goodbye to the cat. The master stood there in silence; you could say he was as frigid as February.

He only burst into tears when he got home.

He cried every day. He counted thirty days in a row.

I know, it's odd, I'm a man, and all that...

At work, they asked him why he was so sad.

'Adulthood came upon me,' he said.

'What? But you're forty years old.'

'You only become an adult when you lose what you truly love,' he explained. 'And it has just happened to me for the first time in my life.' But he didn't add any further information to say who he'd lost, because he found it a bit embarrassing.

So he'd go home, and there was no helping it – he cried.

He wondered how long it would last, and whether he should go and see a psychiatrist, because Holka kept running past under his feet, or he'd hear the parquet creaking joyfully under her paws.

After the thirtieth day came the thirtieth night.

He had a dream. He tells it like this:

'My dad and I are at a seaside resort in Italy. I'm grown-up, and my father is an old man, just as in real life. We're walking towards the sea, we want to go onto the pier, but the whole length of the shoreline there are these long white steps. I think they're made of marble, and they lead straight into the water. Dad starts to go down them. I don't, because I can't swim. Dad has always been extreme, in the past he could put his feet behind his head and walk along ledges, he was always doing tricks like a circus performer. When only his head is still in sight, but he goes on submerging himself, it occurs to me that he's just trying to show off again. "He'll stay underwater for about a minute," I think to myself. He disappears. I wait a minute, then two. I realize that five minutes have passed, but he still hasn't surfaced. I shout four words – "AIUTO, ACQUA, MIO, PADRE" – because I can't put a sentence together in

Italian. People hand me little plastic bottles of mineral water. They think I want water for my father, who has fainted somewhere. I try to call Federica, my Italian girlfriend, to ask what's going to happen, my father's drowning, but I haven't got her number in my phone! Under the name "Fede" there's a gap, I can't see any numbers. I start running towards the town centre, because I know there's a police station there. "AIUTO, ACQUA, MIO, PADRE," I shout at the policemen. One of them asks me my father's first and family name, and I think: "How will an Italian write down something as difficult as Jerzy Szczygieł?" but I tell him. Then the policeman hands me a five-litre bottle of water. I leave the police station, and I know there's nothing, absolutely nothing that can possibly be done anymore. Suddenly, I feel calm. I walk towards the sea and gaze calmly at the steps.'

He got up feeling rested and tranquil. The sense of peace from the dream didn't leave him all day.

That night he came home from work to his empty flat and didn't burst into tears.

And he never cried for the cat again.

A SHORT SKETCH ABOUT
EDI HILA'S NOT THERE

I

A boy is dipping into a pocket encyclopaedia of art. The illustrations are black and white. Someone has sucked out the colours and murdered the pictures. Piero della Francesca – even without the crimson red of Duke Federico da Montefeltro's hat or the rusty gold of the duchess's hair – works on the boy's imagination. Here, the duke looks like his own ghost. In this book, the blue water – a symbol of life – forming the background to his profile looks like ashes. The olive-green earth – a symbol of transience – that's the background for his wife's profile is dark grey. The whole world is familiar with the rich colour of the duke's cylindrical hat, apart from this boy. How would he paint it himself? For the teenager's imagination, the Renaissance in black and white is a provocation.

He has a flair for drawing, and he's lucky, because in Albania only artistic talent gives you the right to study at the sort of school anyone gifted would choose for themselves.

'No other talent gave you that right,' he explains.

'So you had the most useful kind of skill in Albania?'

'Yes, because in all other cases the authorities decided what a young person was going to study. Every high-school graduate was the victim of an act of violence. My father was very eager to become a writer, but the district council decided he'd be an engineer. What luck that, at home, the engineer had a black-and-white Italian encyclopaedia of art published before the war...'

His first ^{NOT THERE} is colour.

2

He graduates from the Academy of Fine Arts in Tirana, and as a promising artist he gets a commission: he's to paint a picture for one of the biggest halls in parliament, known as the People's Assembly. It is to show the People an image of the People planting trees. He decides that *Planting Trees* will look like a joyful dance. He thinks the picture should express the truth and show young people, and that the actual planting could be taking place anywhere and at any time. Girls and boys, some in orange pioneers' scarves, are whirling as they work against a background of green hills. The saplings they're planting are assuming the colour of the sky, an azure blue that's tangled in their young branches. The whole image is pulsating. If it's to be a dance, the brush should dance too. His vibrant brush and its dashing strokes will strengthen the image for the People. The artist doesn't yet know that dashing brushstrokes are pure evil.

For the time being, *Planting Trees* is a great success. It's 1972, and the dictator Enver Hoxha is unexpectedly allowing the nation a breathing space. They're starting to express themselves as they wish, not just through dashing brushstrokes. Books and plays are being written whose authors need not be afraid of failing to be to the Leader's liking. In December, Albanian Radio and Television's 11th Festival of Song is held, and it's different from the previous ten. The female singers perform in long dresses or miniskirts, and the male singers have long hair. The songs aren't about loving the Leader, but simply about love. They play rock music. For the first time ever, there's no hammer, sickle or star built into the set design, but there are rhombuses. Set on top of rectangles. The Leader watches the festival on television for three evenings. He's accompanied by his disciple and planned successor, who asks: 'Aren't song festivals like sugar-coated bonbons with poison inside?' Suddenly, the miniskirts turn out to be bourgeois-revisionist degeneracy. The long hair is defiance. The lack of songs about loving the Leader is sabotage. Singing simply about love is decadence. Playing rock music is unparalleled degeneracy. The geometric shapes on the set are sabotage squared. And the creator of *Planting Trees* is also responsible for the geometry, because he works for television as a set designer. The artists and writers who have taken advantage of the breath of freedom soon realize they have been deceived. The real point of it was for them to expose themselves.

To some extent, the selection of creatives disloyal to the Leader proceeds spontaneously. Now it's clear who doesn't respect the Albanian spirit, because they're drawn to the West. Though for ten years Albania has even been at odds with the Soviet Union, not to mention shutting itself off from all its neighbours. 'The only religion of Albania is Albanianism,' says the Leader.

And now the Albanians tell the creator of *Planting Trees* that 'dashing brushstrokes are not Albanian!' The union of artists and writers holds a meeting. His colleagues advise him to submit self-criticism for the trees and the geometry. He remembers it as a lament expressed by his colleagues (almost all men): he and others are spoiling the tradition, abandoning the rules, they're not resistant to the deluge of art from the West. But above all they haven't resisted being degenerated by foreign influences. So he submits the self-criticism. Because in his – once wonderful – *Planting Trees* there is nothing that should be there.

'Suddenly,' he tells me, 'everything was missing from this painting. I heard that there were no political symbols in it. Not a single one.'

'So?'

'So the picture's biggest problem is that it's realistic. It presents human optimism in a lucid and direct manner.'

'Isn't that a good thing?' I suggest. 'Optimistic people planting trees for their country...'

'But it isn't revolutionary optimism. Human optimism can be expressed in art through realism, and that's what my picture does. Revolutionary optimism is realism plus communism. And that is not there. Then there was a second meeting at my workplace, meaning the television studio, where they criticized me even more fiercely. A plenum of the Party's Central Committee took the decision to punish me, the artist, by sending me to the working class for re-education, for an indefinite period. I started hauling sacks at poultry plants.'

His second ^{NOT THERE} is the right kind of optimism.

3

He draws in pencil or ink, on very small cards – so he can take them out of the plant in his pocket. *Counting Sacks, Three Unloaders, Women Labourers Transporting Sacks...* Their faces are swollen and deformed. The first thing we see is their ominous eyes, definitely devoid of any kind of optimism at all. Tragedy, but without pathos. You could say it's the tragedy that's naturally inherent in such a fate. He thinks he drew female workers resting on sacks who are cheerful, but I can't see anything in the picture to confirm that, even by examining the women's faces under a magnifying glass.

The labourers at the factory know that a re-educated man is working as a loader and unloader. One of them asks him: 'What are you hauling sacks for?' He listens to the reply, but interrupts it with a question: 'If we've been lugging these sacks all our lives, are we being punished too?'

The punished artist locks the drawings away in a drawer. And so it goes for the next ten years. Now he's deprived of a past. Objectively, of course, he has one, but he can't officially refer to it. For example, he can live on quiet memories of the one and only trip he has ever made abroad, to Florence – and the paintings at the Uffizi, which have stayed in his mind in colour.

Who knows if stronger memories might not come under article 55 of the penal code: agitation and propaganda against the state and the government, which carries a penalty ranging from ten years in prison to a death sentence? It's better not to mention the past. But also better not to judge the present. For instance, article 55 includes the opinion that shoes in Albania are flimsy, or that there's a lack of shoes in the shops.

Among those who end up in prison is the artist Edison Gjergo. (When he comes out, he'll fall victim to alcoholism and will die of it.) In 1971, he produced a large oil painting, *The Epic of the Morning Stars* – a famous-infamous picture, like *Planting Trees*. In it, he depicted some people listening to an old man playing the fiddle at dawn. The figures in the picture are appropriate: soldiers, farm workers and labourers. Unfortunately, the picture contains pessimism and is too reminiscent of the style of Chagall. And why are they listening to a fiddler at dawn, and not during the day? What are they hiding? What are they afraid of? Maybe they're plotting?

No one knows who might fall foul of whom, and who will organize a committee against whom, but it's sure to come to the studio to scrutinize the daubs and sculptures. The inspectors of culture – as representatives of communist values – enter houses without warning. The state generously gives the artist up to six months free from state service, for instance from painting signs or posters, to create a work. But then that work must be shown to the state.

The author of *Planting Trees* reckons he's better off than the creator of *The Epic of the Morning Stars*, because he's not in prison.

'And best of all,' he stresses, 'those committees stopped coming to see me.'

'How come?'

'I was no longer an artist, I was just a sack porter. As I'd been convicted, I didn't exist for them anymore. I wasn't there. Nobody checked up on me! And I felt truly liberated. I could paint without inspection, like a real, free artist. Then, at last, I had a sense of being alive...'

His third ^{NOT THERE} is his own self.*

---

* We are sitting (on 3 March 2018) by the window of a large pavilion, on a riverbank. Edi Hila is gazing at the Vistula. For the first time in his 74-year-old life – in this very pavilion – a retrospective exhibition of his work is being held. Pictures have been brought together from every period of his creative life. In a short while (also for the first time in Hila's life), a professor from the Academy of Fine Arts in Tirana – Edi Hila – will show the public around his exhibition in person.

After the fall of the Leader, he started to paint the suburbs, illegal extensions, houses built without involving an architect, and unfinished constructions. He was recreating chaos. He named these cycles *Threat*, *Landscapes of Transformation*, *Peripheries*, and *Roadside Structures*. Here, hidden in the bushes, is an unfinished house with no ground floor. There's just an abandoned upper floor standing on its columns. Perhaps the owners emigrated? Here's a series named *Martyrs of the Nation Boulevard* (in Tirana), featuring edifices erected by, first, the monarchy, then the fascists, then the communists, and now the victorious democrats. Dismal, lifeless façades dominate an empty space, all the strong colours have fled from the pictures, and everything's sprinkled in artist's dust, grey or brown. Edi Hila invites us on his guided tour. He stops in front of a large picture, *Boulevard 6* (2015), in which he has boldly painted the headquarters of the chairman of the council of ministers as a black rectangle.

'Just imagine,' he adds with a laugh, 'this picture was actually displayed in the foyer of this very building.'

'What did the prime minister have to say about your painting of his HQ?'

'The prime minister? He was delighted! He's Edi Rama, my former student and fellow painter.'

A STAR AMONG VILLAS

Mr and Mrs Müller wanted to live in beauty.

Beauty is not given once and for all. And those who want it only for themselves, even if they paid for it, will be punished.

Milada and František Müller can't have foreseen this.

PART ONE

The Villa Müller soon became a star among villas. The Prague newspapers wrote that it was the only house in the city whose construction everyone was 'following with appreciation and interest'. The new functionalism and modernism in architecture meant that houses were no longer a mystery.

When you look at any building, it's more than likely that by studying the arrangement of the windows on the façade you can guess the layout of the rooms inside, and even imagine their interiors.

But examining the façade of the Müllers' house will hardly tell you anything at all.

Apparently not a single room in the house is on the same level as any other.

'To get from the dining room to the library we must go down two steps, then up eight, and down three again,' reports the *Prager Tagblatt* on 22 January 1930.

The designer of the villa is Adolf Loos from Vienna, a famous architect, though self-taught. One of the ladies who visited the Villa Müller immediately after they moved in on 30 May 1930 wrote in the guest book that now there was a new aristocracy in Europe – those who ordered a house from Loos.

'War and illness can come along, and no one can control them. But apart from those two things, I believe that anyone who lives in this house and doesn't feel extremely happy doesn't deserve to be alive. I've travelled a lot, I've seen a lot, but I have NEVER seen a house with such inner sunshine, with such internal and external beauty,' the Danish writer Karin Michaëlis wrote in the guest book. 'I feel as if this villa was erected by two builders – Adolf Loos and Sheer Happiness.'

Adolf Loos orchestrates a surprise.

To reach the salon from the small vestibule, the guest goes up a narrow staircase. At once, he feels as if he's being squeezed through the constricted throat of a snake.

First the staircase leads him up, but soon after it unexpectedly takes him down, onto the parquet floor of the salon. The guest is spat out of the claustrophobic gorge of the staircase into an infinite space. The contrast between the restricted bowel of the staircase and the sweep of the salon is stunning. The person entering feels as though they've suddenly stepped on stage.

There's no point, explains the architect, in entering the salon the ordinary way by simply opening a door – then there would be no effect. But passing through the claustrophobic staircase, up and down, makes the room seem even more spacious than its dimensions would imply.

Only here do we understand Loos' view that the house 'is to be a stage for acting out the great drama of life'.

Someone upbraids him for making the stairs as narrow as the steps to a cabin on a ship. He regards this as a very great compliment and exclaims: 'Exactly! A ship is the best model for a modern house! There, every scrap of space is used to the maximum. A staircase isn't for couples to pass each other on!'

Adolf Loos tailors the house to fit.

Milada Müllerová is small, and her husband is tall. According to rumour, there's half a metre between them. In their wedding photos, you can't see the difference, because someone had the bright idea of seating the groom in an armchair, while the bride is standing next to it – that way, he wouldn't be quite so tall or she quite so small. In others the bride is sitting with the ladies, and the groom is standing with the gentlemen; once again, we don't notice the apparently acute difference, though if you look carefully you can see that the bride is the only lady whose shoes do not touch the floor.

The architect designs the villa in such a way that when Mrs Müllerová is to appear to her guests in the salon she will have no unfortunate collision with persons taller than her. In her own house, she can look tall, and can even choose to tower over the company. She's a modest woman, so she towers over them tastefully, without effrontery.

How is this possible?

The salon is next door to the boudoir and the dining room. The main wall that links it with the other rooms is not in one piece, but more like a Swiss cheese. It has gaps, niches, supporting pillars, landings and plinths. We feel as if the interior of this house were multiplying before our eyes.

And it's the landings that give Mrs Müllerová social opportunities. She doesn't have to descend to the floor in the salon. She can emerge from her boudoir or the dining room, stop on the landing and quite naturally appear above her guests. She'll be seen and heard.

High above the salon ceiling, we can see a window to the boudoir. It looks like the window in a train compartment. Mrs Müllerová can push it up and observe the guests in the salon.

The architect takes her height into consideration in the boudoir too. The room is small, but it's on two levels. When the lady is higher up and the gentleman lower down, she can look him straight in the eyes.

Adolf Loos singles out the father.

On one of the plinths built into the grand salon wall the architect places a bronze bust of Mr Müller's father, Antonín. It was he who founded the company in Plzeň that is later owned by his son, František. During the reign of the Habsburg monarchy, this company, Müller & Kapsa, was a front runner in the use of reinforced concrete. It built bridges, factories, a church, and also this villa.

From his plinth, the father keeps watch over the entire salon.

Adolf Loos devises clever solutions.

An invisible shower on the roof. Despite being outside, Mrs Müllerová can stand beneath it completely naked. From under the shower she can see the entire neighbourhood, but nobody can see her.

The outbox in Mr Müller's desk. On the right-hand side of the tabletop there's a long, narrow slot. Whenever Müller has addressed a letter, he drops it into the slot, and the next day the servant opens a little door in the side of the desk and takes the correspondence to the post office.

The expanding tabletop. In the dining room, there's a round tabletop on a fat wooden pedestal that seats six people. When a wooden ring is attached around the tabletop, twelve diners can sit at it. There's a second, spare ring, thanks to which a table for eighteen guests can come into being.

A secret passage in a closet. During dinner, the guests might get a fright: on two sides of the dining room there are mahogany closets; one of them conceals the dinner service that came with Mrs Müllerová's dowry, but the other one will suddenly open, and a footman will step out. It contains a hidden door to a meal station, where the cook puts the dishes that are ready to be served.

Safety cords. In the bathroom, there's a system for switching the lights on and off with the help of pull cords – so that a wet hand cannot come into contact with electricity.

The chairs and armchairs in the salon. There are ten of them, each different from the others. 'One shall choose one's type of seat according to mood and need!' announces the architect.

Aquaria as lamps. In the salon, we don't have to switch on the globe lights hanging from the ceiling. Instead, the intimate glow from the fireplace and two fish tanks built into the wall keeps us company.

A living loudspeaker. During parties in the salon, a musical quartet is seated on a sofa in the boudoir. Then the inside window overlooking the salon is raised, and the guests can hear the music as if from a loudspeaker fixed to the ceiling.

A living postcard. On the flat roof of the villa, right at the very edge, the architect is forced to place a rather tall chimney. To make sure it won't fall over, Loos builds it into a frame that surrounds a view of Hradčany.

Adolf Loos runs riot with materials.

The walls and furniture in the boudoir are overlaid with lemonwood the colour of dark honey. When the sun shines through the windowpane, the boudoir is like the inside of a piece of amber.

The dining-room table has a top cut from grey syenite. Under no circumstances can it ever be covered with a tablecloth. 'The finest tablecloth is a beautiful tabletop,' he informs the Müllers.

Loos covers the walls of the master bedroom with French wallpaper the colour of sand with blue scenes. They represent life in a land by the sea, based on eighteenth-century illustrations by Claude-Joseph Vernet. And to avoid obscuring the scenes in the drawings, all the light switches are made of glass.

The salon space, despite being modern, is elevated by what has always elevated refined spaces: marble. The walls in the salon are partly clad in rare marble facing – it's Cipolin de Saillon marble, tinged green with bands of grey onyx.

Adolf Loos introduces colour.

The guest crossing the threshold of the villa should at once feel pleasure, so the entire corridor just past the door is clad in glass painted green. The architect thus refers to a colour that guests bring with them under their eyelids – the entire Střešovice district is bursting with greenery.

In each room, one should feel that sorrow is denied entry to this house. So in every window throughout the house all the curtains are golden yellow and made of silk. On gloomy days, they are to make it feel as if the sun were trying to get inside the villa.

Loos believes in Piet Mondrian's theory of pure colour, and thus in blue, red and yellow. A combination of these colours is the only way to create balance between individuality and universality, in other words, between two opposing aspects of life. In the two rooms occupied by the Müllers' daughter Eva stands lacquered furniture in those very colours. Because only in this grouping of colours will the little girl grow up to be a happy and healthy woman.

In the kitchen, the architect introduces only one of Mondrian's colours. All the furniture in it is deep yellow.

Adolf Loos imprisons the porcelain.

One of the cupboards in the boudoir looks like a cage. It's a glazed cabinet made of bronze, standing in a corner. Only here can Mrs Müllerová keep her beloved porcelain vases and figurines, all gold borders and Secession curves. As if the creator of the Müllers' life wants everything decorative to be shut away in one place, kept separate from the rest of the house.

So that none of this kitsch will have a chance of spreading around the villa.

Humanity spends too much energy on adornment, he believes. 'Ornament is wasted labour power and hence wasted health,' Adolf Loos wrote in his 1908 essay 'Ornament and Crime'.

He never abandons his views. He maintains that cultural evolution depends on eliminating ornament from everyday objects. He thought that by making this statement he would provide everyone with a reason to be satisfied. 'But no one thanked me. People were dejected. It made them sad to think they could no longer create decoration,' he notes.

Hence the cage, perhaps.

Apparently, there were several objects that the owners of the house only fetched from their flat in Plzeň after the architect's death, because he would not agree to their presence in the villa in his lifetime.

The engineer who worked with Loos recalled that when the architect saw him in a café leafing through a magazine about interior decorating, *Innen-Dekoration*, he tore it from his hands and said: 'Don't look at that or you'll ruin yourself.'

Adolf Loos grounds the sofas.

As an experienced interior designer, he knows that the residents of the house might rearrange the furniture contrary to his intentions. And so he has the sofas in the vestibule, salon, boudoir and dining room fixed permanently in place. In niches from which they cannot be moved.

Adolf Loos gives in on the issue of a divan.

Unfortunately, the leather sofas in the master's study are great for sitting, but completely unsuitable for lying down – they are too short and uncomfortable for tall Mr Müller.

When it turns out the master of the house has nowhere to take his post-prandial nap – and in houses of a certain standard no one goes to bed in the afternoon – Loos agrees with great reluctance to a divan in the dressing room.

František Müller is able to repay his dictator. For instance, he pays him several times for the same thing, and when the architect suddenly telegraphs from Paris to say that he's out of money and has nothing to settle his hotel bill, Mr Müller sends a car from Prague with cash.

Adolf Loos is ruthless towards the cook.

Granted, the kitchen does have two windows, but positioned so high up that the cook cannot look out of them. According to Loos, if she gazes at the street she won't be focused on her job.

Adolf Loos (on behalf of František Müller) obliges the servants.

One of the engineers working with Loos and Müller insists that the servants must have their own rooms in the villa, rather than live on top of each other in the basement or travel to work.

'Mr Müller, you will be three people spread out over thirteen rooms and you'll breed a houseful of class enemies,' he said, in an effort to persuade the boss.

To which Müller says that if the cook comes to live with them, she'll oversleep, arrive in the kitchen unwashed and unkempt, and will tidy her hair at work. 'For reasons of hygiene that's unacceptable. But if she lives in her own home, she'll have to think about her appearance before she leaves it.'

However, the engineer sticks to his guns.

Loos accuses him of playing the role of father to the poor. 'I'm keen to see a shred of humanity here,' the engineer argues. 'And besides,' he adds, 'I've been sent a book from America about rich men's villas, and over there the servants have their own rooms with bathrooms.'

The American argument closes the debate.

PART TWO

Mr and Mrs Müller wanted to live in beauty, and all Prague was behind them.

To this day, the villa is overgrown not just with ivy, but also with urban legends. I walked around the Střešovice district and neighbouring Ořechovka, where I talked to neighbours and admirers of the house. The myths about it are as follows:

- when the communists came to power in Czechoslovakia the house was requisitioned by the state;
- the daughter hated the villa so much that at the first opportunity she fled abroad and never returned;
- the daughter, who had the balanced colours of happiness in her room, became mentally ill;
- straight after, František Müller was poisoned by toxic gas in the boiler room;

(An unfortunate accident? On the very day when he burned all the documents relating to the villa's construction, apart from the accounts?)

- a brothel exclusively for senior army officers was opened in the house;
- it was a hostel for Arab students;
- the house was occupied by a Centre for Marxism–Leninism;

(Milada Müllerová became the cleaner there. The communists allowed her to walk about her own house only in office hours. Then she was locked in the smallest room, used for a maid.

This room had been her own invention: a maid, she had said, doesn't need a larger one.

The irony of fate.

Now Milada had to fit in it with all her paintings and furniture.)

· no, Mrs Müllerová lived in her boudoir and only looked through that 'railway' window to watch the communists working;

(The security service planted a young woman in the house, an art historian, who first convinced the lonely, exhausted Mrs Müllerová that she was her cousin, and then moved in with her. This functionary was to monitor what she did with the works of art, which the state could not legally appropriate – and to write reports.

The fake cousin induced Müllerová to give her some items as gifts, and passed them on to the authorities.)

· Mrs Müllerová died of a heart attack from fright when the Red Army entered Prague and occupied her house.

So much for the legends.

(I decided to track down the 'fake cousin'. It was easy to establish her maiden name. The house's documents include a declaration she wrote in 1959, which says that for helping her sick, ageing aunt she received five oil paintings, a rug, a dinner service for twelve, a snuffbox, earrings, a necklace and so on.

It turns out that she left the country in the 1960s and never returned. But a woman with her surname was listed as an art expert on the 'About' page of the website for an art gallery in the West. So I've sent them a letter…)

It is 2009.

A white-haired old woman who walks on crutches is sitting at the table in the Müllers' dining room. Marie Lauermannová is ninety-four. The last time she was here was sixty-six years ago. She feels uneasy, she's clearly nervous.

She has come with her sister's grandson's wife. Marie's sister, called Granny in the conversation that follows, is two years her junior. They are the villa's longest living neighbours – their house is only separated from the Müllers' by a fence. Unfortunately, her sister is incapable of walking unaided. They moved into the house next door to the villa in 1928, when Marie was thirteen, her sister eleven, and Müller and Loos had just started construction.

'Oh, how I've longed to come here once more before I die,' she says excitedly, and lists the staff employed by the neighbours. 'They had a gardener, a maid, a governess and a cook – she was old and tall, I can see her clear as day. They had a chauffeur too – he lived here, in Střešovice – and a footman. I used to stare at him like a fool. We had a gardener and a maid too, but no footman. And the Müllers' footman used to run around the garden in polished patent leather shoes. I'm sure you know the type from the old silent films.'

When Mrs Lauermannová realizes she's dealing with someone who is 'writing a book about the villa', she becomes cagey. We talk, but she's not very forthcoming.

Next day her sister's grandson's wife sends me an 'interview with Great-Aunt Marie'. She had done her best to ask her the same questions again, immediately afterwards that same day (8 June 2009), 'otherwise I'd have forgotten what you asked'.

Indeed, Marie Lauermannová opens before us a whole props room full of desirable details, soon to be forgotten for ever.

Cousin: 'Granny said Mr Müller stammered, is that right?'

Mrs Lauermannová: 'I don't know about that. Did she ever talk to him?'

'She must have done, or how would she know?'

'That's very interesting, because I never spoke to him, and I'm older. What would he have had to talk to your granny about? In the past neighbours weren't in the habit of shouting over the fence or from window to window. It was a different era. And they were the elite, so it was quite impossible. We might greet each other in the street, exchange a few words, but we didn't run round to the neighbours' for coffee, the way people do nowadays. For us, entering their house was out of the question. I'm wondering where and when she could have talked to him...'

'So you didn't visit each other?'

'It simply wasn't appropriate. They were from the "upper ten thousand", as they say these days. And they only invited people who were like them. We were rich too, but they were a decidedly better class.'

'And when was the first time you went inside the villa?'

'The first and last time – it was March 1943. I know the precise date, because it was after our father's death. I went there with Mummy and your granny. Mrs Müllerová invited us. She had no other occupation except to invite people.'

'But Granny said that Mrs Müllerová didn't regard herself as better than others. Though her mother flaunted her wealth...'

'That's not true. Both of them were always very elegantly dressed. Of course, we were too. There was no question of leaving the house without gloves and a hat, those little hats with a veil in front were in fashion then, I had one of those too. But to go out without stockings, the way they do today?! Not even a skivvy would have taken the liberty. At the Müllers' the staff always wore gloves to serve the food. The laundered ones used to hang over there, on a line, and how many there were! Both ladies always went about in real karakul coats, none of those cheaper foxes with the paws around your neck.'

'And do you know what happened to Mr Müller in the end?'

'Yes, he was asphyxiated by toxic gas from the boiler room.'

'And what was he doing in the boiler room, if he had staff for everything?'

'But he wasn't in the boiler room. He was sitting in his study. He liked to read over a glass of wine. He was poisoned in that position.'

'Didn't he smell the toxic gas?'

'He fell asleep and didn't notice it. At least that's what was said at the time. They burned coke. We had two American coke-fired ovens too, but we cooked using coal. At the Müllers' the whole kitchen was modern, with electricity – we didn't have that. There was one morning when they didn't have any electricity, and their cook came running to our house with a raw chicken to ask if we'd roast it for them.'

'And what happened to their mum? She came to a bad end too.'

'Mrs Müllerová's mother was killed by a tram. She didn't live here to begin with, but somewhere in the city centre. It was only a few years later that she moved into the villa, upstairs. And that time... she'd been to the theatre. She got off the tram, but her view was blocked by her umbrella and she didn't notice another tram coming the other way. Some people carried her into the villa's garage and rang for an ambulance. In the process they managed to rob her of all she had. And the Müllers were sitting upstairs, not knowing a thing. I don't know if she died in the ambulance or at the hospital.'

'That's dreadful, they robbed her while she was still alive?'

'Yes, it's dreadful, but in those days that was common. And under the Germans, it was quite usual for people to go down into the shelter, and if anyone came a cropper and was killed in the street, they were robbed afterwards by the people who came back out of the shelters. During a war, people change into hyenas.'

'Did the family have any animals?'

'Mrs Müllerová had Pekinese dogs. And a beehive on the roof. That was a nightmare, because we had a pear tree growing by the gate to our villa, and when the pears were ripe it was impossible to enter the property because of the swarm of bees.'

'And what did Mrs Müllerová and her daughter do all day?'

'Nothing.'

'But they must have filled their time somehow. What were their occupations?'

'Well, the things the wealthy classes did in those days. The mother invited her friends over for a chat, and went to art galleries. Eva learned languages. But they didn't do any work. My mother had no trouble lending our cook a hand, and I used to help the maid to wash the steps, and we'd have a natter. At the Müllers', that was impossible. Mrs Müllerová was even driven to church by the chauffeur.'

'Here, to our church? Round the corner?'

'No, she went somewhere beyond Hradčany, but she could have got there on foot too.'

'Granny said that Mrs Müllerová worked in her rock garden, and that it gave her pleasure.'

'No. I never saw her work. None of the Müllers worked. She liked the rockery, she used to order plants for it from Holland. Kinds that aren't familiar here. But mainly she supervised the gardener. I never saw her do any work.'

'Did she go to the shops?'

'Of course not, the cook did the shopping. Except you didn't buy things like nowadays. For instance, the cook would run to the butcher's for meat, and when she was on her way back, the wooden cart with the milk churns would be coming up the street, pulled by a dog. People would run out of their houses with jugs and get as much milk as they needed... It wouldn't have been at all suitable for Mrs Müllerová to buy things that way.'

'And what do you know about the daughter?'

'Eva was about ten years younger than me. She must be around eighty, if she's still alive. They had a big problem with her marriage. Is it appropriate to tell the writer that?'

'Yes. He knows about it.'

'She found a suitor whom Mrs Müllerová didn't like at all. Nor did Mr Müller, but the mother was right off him. He was a manufacturer, Materna – paints. Varnishes. Veneers. They probably had someone even richer in mind. So Eva got married in secret. The Müllers weren't at the wedding. The young couple sent them a gigantic azalea and an announcement to say they were now married. And they left for France, then Canada. They had one son. That grandson of the Müllers' visited me recently.'

'How recently?'

'About twenty years ago. He was looking for the Villa Müller. Because he'd never been here, and didn't even know what it looks like. He came to see us and we had a bit of a chat.'

'So Mrs Müllerová's life was not a success. Her mother and husband both died in tragic accidents, and her daughter went away. There's nothing to envy her for.'

'Fame and cash are like litter and ash. And that was such a rich and famous family. Müllerová ended up a lonely lady, abandoned by all. She had no one left but the dog.'

'And how did she live after the war?'

'The Soviets came and we were all given someone to put up. Two colonels and a general lived at our house. No one asked us if we were willing to do it, they just billeted them and that was that. They used to eat fish, pulling off the heads and flinging them over there, into the corner of the room. Horrible. And they never stopped drinking. At the time there was no sugar, but they brought in a whole garageful of it. I don't know where they got it from. There were Russians next door too. Mrs Müllerová kept hens in the laundry – she'd put a plank out of a small window so they could come and go as they pleased. The Russkies clubbed them all to death and ate them. She also had a rooster, but he was a devil. Once she went out in that hat with the veil, and for some reason that veil antagonized the rooster and he jumped on her head.'

'Do you know how she died?'

'That I don't know. Somehow, the place gradually became deserted. When she was alone there, she started coming up to the fence to talk. She hadn't the strength to take care of things anymore, she needed help. My husband used to bring her ration cards from the administration. There were ration cards from

1939 until 1953. The villa was abandoned and the garden went to seed. And the worst time was when communists infested the Müllers' house.'

'What was so bad about it?'

'When the sun shone, they used to drag those valuable chairs onto the terrace and sit around in them. But they never took them back inside afterwards. They left them outside in the rain!'

(It has been several weeks, and the foreign gallery hasn't replied. No one picks up the phone either. The 'fake cousin's' surname is not very common in the Czech Republic, and there's a man with the same name listed in the Prague phone book.

Yes, he's her brother.

Yes, he can easily give me the phone number.)

It's still 2009.

Eugen Stumpf says that yesterday was his eightieth birthday. He receives me in a room full of old pictures and sophisticated objects. For the past twenty-five years he has been a translator of cookery books from German. He started off as a sculptor. 'He was a subtle and talented boy. He sculpted with great feeling. He didn't believe in himself, he didn't trust himself. He didn't believe he could one day be a great sculptor,' is what Vladimír Preclík, another sculptor, wrote about him.

'Do you know the principle that guided Loos in designing the villa?' he asks excitedly on the doorstep. And answers himself: 'The interior must be designed in such a way that an antique amphora can be placed beside a painting by Picasso.'

'How did you first come upon the villa?' I ask.

'Just a moment and I'll tell you, but first I have to say that it's the most beautiful place I've ever been in the whole world. As Mrs Müllerová always used to say to me: "Evžen, this is a house that could never be boring." The way the spaces are entirely interwoven... the vestibule, where the walls are painted matt white... Do you know how that matt colour was obtained?'

'Not entirely...'

'All the veneer, I'll have you know, had to be gently sanded, because in those days matt paints did not exist. First, everything was painted in gloss white, and then it was rubbed with sandpaper. And that was done three times: painting and sanding. If the workmen doing the sanding made just one tiny cut in the wood, one scratch, the whole panel had be taken off the wall and reinstalled. Loos couldn't tolerate those cuts...'

'And you ended up at the villa...'

'Wait a moment and I'll tell you, I just want to ask if you felt the sense of theatre in there? You go down a few steps and suddenly you find yourself not in the middle of a large room, but to one side of it, right by the wall – and you have to look around you. And at that moment you're being manipulated by the architect...'

'And you were in the villa...'

'I'll tell you all about it, I'd just like to know if it was sunny or cloudy the day you were in the boudoir?'

'Does it matter?'

'Of course! In the boudoir, when the sun is shining, the wood crystallizes optically, as if it were transparent. The craftsmanship in that house is fantastic!'

'And the first time you knocked at the door...'

'Forgive my importunity, but did you notice that the marble in the salon doesn't look like stone at all? It has veins of onyx, like the patterns in wood... And in a very pleasant shade. That's why the marble doesn't look cold. Of course, you know that we're not dealing with blocks of marble that form part of the wall, but with cladding?'

'I know they're marble panels. How did you first become intere—'

'And that's extraordinary for Loos. I often think about it. He couldn't bear anything inauthentic!'

'That marble was intended for another house he had designed, but apparently the owners didn't like it, so Loos used it for the Müllers' house instead. But there was slightly too little of it, so each of the original slabs of marble was split to obtain two that were identical, but thinner.'

'You've done your homework!'

'I'm a great admirer of the villa too, and I'd like to cast a little light on the private history of the house. So if you could tell me how you ended up there...'

'I'll get onto that, but let me just add that for the dining room, on either side of the window, in the corners of the room, Loos made these copper cabinets with glazed fronts for flowers that stood behind the glass. The ideal place for cactuses. Later, they removed the flowers and put shells and butterflies in there. What a fine sight!'

'And when was the first time you saw those cabinets?'

'One day, the villa was to be taken over by military counter-intelligence, to serve as a secret base. That was when I met Mrs Müllerová. It was early 1955, and they were about to move her to a single room in the suburbs, to a hut with bare wooden floorboards!'

'To what?'

'To a small space with bare wooden floorboards! Can you imagine? And I helped her.'

'How?'

'You won't believe me, but it all has to do with Sartre, his *Roads to Freedom* and a girl with a big bust. I'll tell you the story, but I forgot to ask if you know what the sofa cushions at the Villa Müller were stuffed with?'

'No.'

'Feathers! Real feathers. So you don't know everything!'

'What's that about Sartre and the girl with the big bust?'

'I was studying pottery and sculpture. One of my classmates was on his way to college, bringing me a book my whole generation was eager to read – *The Roads to Freedom* by Sartre. It was cold, he was wearing a sheepskin coat, and he had the book wrapped in paper underneath it. Then the busty girl from our year boarded the same tram. That was her nickname among the students – Busty – for pity's sake, I won't tell you her real name. Later on she moved to Poland for good, and designed some monuments in your country. "What have you got there, Háječek?" she asked, because she realized he had something under his coat. "I'm taking Evžen the new Gorky," Háječek lied. When they got to college, the silly man put the packet down on a radiator, the book slipped out and fell on the floor. The wrapping came off, revealing Sartre. At first, Busty was dumbstruck, as if paralysed, and then she went nuts. What an insult to Czechoslovakia's working people! What she found most offensive was that Háječek had used Gorky to conceal Sartre. Somehow it blew over, and I never imagined she'd report it to the college authorities. And then came an exam, and they asked if I'd read Sholokhov's *And Quiet Flows the Don*. I'm unable to tell a lie, so I said I hadn't. To which the lecturer said: "You've had time for Sartre, but not Sholokhov?" All hell broke loose! They held a meeting, they threw me out of the Party, which I'd been in for a year, and they expelled me from the college. But they never bothered to ask me if I agreed with Sartre!'

'What does this have to do with the villa?'

'Everything. Because if it wasn't for that incident, Mrs Müllerová would have gone to live in the hut with a bare wooden floor!'

'All right, please go on.'

'Professor Wagner told me to come and see him. "Evžen," he said, "you've got the army ahead of you whatever. Why don't you just enlist? Then it'll all quieten down, you'll restart your education, and you'll be back at college." For me, who was longing to be a sculptor, it was a catastrophe. But in my second year of military service I was assigned as a clerk to the office in charge of real estate in Prague. At the time the army owned lots of accommodation, which was not administered by the city but by the ministry of defence. I was taken on by a captain as his secretary. He was a miner from Ostrava and he couldn't type. Not at all. On top of which he had a horrible wife who slapped him around the chops. He told me so himself. They had four children. He was very happy to have me working for him, because he was always having to sneak off home – to do the laundry and ironing. All of a sudden I had turned from an enemy of the system into a someone at the ministry of defence. The first person I helped was called— anyway, never mind about that, let's get onto the Villa Müller. The problem of General Lomský cropped up. He was already living in a villa – stolen of course, because the houses were being taken away from capitalists and occupied by communists. But there were forty steps up to his villa; the general's wife had just had a baby, and she couldn't get the pram up those steps. Our office was to sort out another house for him. The general and his wife went for a walk through the smart Ořechovka district and chose a grand villa, which was already occupied of course. By four families of high-up communists. My captain and I began to work out a plan for moving them to other houses, so that Lomský could move in there. It turned out that for his sake eleven families would have to move. The captain was tearing his hair out. We got the idea of writing about it, unofficially of course, to the president of the republic, Novotný. As the Villa Müller had just been chosen as the HQ for counter-intelligence, I'd already been there in an official capacity and met its unusual owner, so I wrote the villa into the letter we sent to the president.'

'What do you mean, you wrote the villa into your letter?'

'I wrote that it was absurd for counter-intelligence to have such an eye-catching house. How could secret services be based in a building straight out of the architecture guidebook, a villa that tourists came to visit, at least to see it from the outside? This house should only be used for cultural purposes. For the benefit of the working people. President Novotný put a stop to the general's move, but also halted the acquisition of the Villa Müller by the army. And so in March 1955 it was given to the Museum of Applied Arts. If it weren't for Sartre and Busty, the villa would have been doomed. For my part in this, Mrs Müllerová gave me a well-worn rug.'

'Oh dear, that's a bit mean...'

'She also sold me a fabulous seventeenth-century jug, hand-hammered bronze. She was selling everything off. She was living there in awful poverty, she had no income or pension, all she could do was get rid of things. So buying that jug or anything else meant extending Mrs Müllerová's life. The communists had clouted her with an incredible tax bill – a so-called millionaires' tax, which was designed to ruin all the rich people in the country. She had no heating. I remember that in winter she looked like an old Jew, she wore a large cap inside the house all the time. In January it only got up to fourteen degrees Celsius in there – I know because we once measured the temperature together. It wasn't until the Museum of Applied Arts turned the villa into its warehouse that it got some heating. They kept the freezing cold in check. But the authorities soon came to the conclusion that the museum director was protecting the wife of a millionaire, and the building was transferred to a pedagogical publisher. And as for them – they were a tribe of vandals.'

'The pedagogues?'

'The editors. Can you imagine, they unscrewed Loos' door handles, threw them in the dustbin, and installed ordinary ones! Mrs Müllerová showed me. "Evžen," she said, 'look what I pulled out of the rubbish today..." The Müllers had excellent taste, not at all pretentious. Well, the one thing that, to my taste, was a tad nouveau riche, but just a tad, were those two fish tanks. Did you know that one of them contained salt water, and the other fresh water?'

'But let's get back to Mrs Müllerová.'

'You have to know that she spoke French and English perfectly. She could quote Shakespeare in the original, but would never do it to show off, it was always natural. She never complained about her lot or said anything bad about others. She had great class. She ate nothing but bread and jam, because they kept raising those taxes of hers. I think she lived on a single dream. That was what kept her going.'

'What was it?'

'That the villa would be turned into a museum, and she would be employed there as a guide.'

(I call the 'fake cousin'. She lives in a small village in the north of Italy. She's surprised someone has found her, forty years after she left Czechoslovakia. I say I'd very much like to come and see her, because she knew a person who is of great interest to me – Mrs Müllerová.

Oh dear, she says, it's very hard to get to her place. First you'd have to travel to Austria, then half a day by train...

I'd be happy to send her my book about the Czechs, would she please just give me the address? Once I've got it, I type it into Google Earth and I can see her house. I'm looking at your street now from a satellite, I say, and it'd be no problem for me to get there. There's so much greenery around your house... I'd love to see it. But will you please talk to me?

I think I'll take a look at your book first, she says.

At least she didn't say no.)

The ageing Milada Müllerová floated around her own former villa like a phantom. That's the picturesque way Eugen Stumpf put it. I imagine her at night, when the people who work there have left the building, roaming the corridors and touching every door handle.

On 8 November 1965, ten years after the outsiders moved in, she drew up a detailed list of crimes committed against her house:

- The varnish on the front door is chipped;
- a doorhandle has lost its black ivory knob;
- parts of the green glass in the corridor walls are broken;
- several oak steps are missing;
- the stairs have been waxed with a polish that contains water, but this kind of oak can't bear water, and should be cleaned with sawdust;
- the boiler in the bathroom has been removed without a new one being installed, so there's no hot water, and the cold water flows very slowly;
- the locks from the three closets for dirty laundry have all disappeared, leaving holes in their place;
- there are irremovable stains on the furniture in the cloakrooms, caused by placing wet glasses, used teaspoons and fruit peel on them;
- there is a large hole in the door of one of the children's rooms from when the handle was replaced;
- in the other children's room, a telephone line has been installed, causing damage to almost every wall;
- in both children's rooms, the red linoleum has been cleaned with a strong soap concentrate, which has deprived the floor of its colour;
- the lamps designed by Loos have all been removed and replaced by fluorescent lights, which are completely unsuited to this style;
- the lampshades have ended up on the floor of the

ironing room, where they have been lying in dust and
dirt;

- the Japanese lantern has disappeared from the
  summer dining room;
- next to the summer dining room there's a second
  guest room, where Comrade Dejmková is living
  illegally;
- the veneer in the vestibule – sanded three times to
  produce a matt effect – has had strips peeled off it in
  many places;
- two of the lampshades in the vestibule ceiling are
  broken;
- the bench that was in the vestibule is now in the corridor by the kitchen;
- the baskets for used umbrellas have come apart;
- the furniture from the salon (all of it!) has been put
  in a bathroom, which is not the best place for it;
- the aquaria (empty) have a bronze grille on top, on
  which various heavy objects have been placed;

and so on...

'In the boudoir, where I live,' wrote Milada Müllerová, 'despite
the fact that I have a broken leg and am disabled, as a result of
orders from higher up, all my light fuses have been switched
off. So I have to shine a small torch to be able to move around
in there. I use this room for sleeping and for storing my

considerable collection of paintings. This collection is constantly being borrowed by the National Gallery and sent abroad (currently to Russia), but whenever the pictures are moved there is damage to the veneer in the boudoir, which is made of Indian lemonwood. The room next to the boudoir is the study, full of books, and it has been spared, because I am the only person who occupies it. I stress: the items I have in the house, whether made of porcelain or stone, and also the paintings, are important works, essential to the whole of human culture. They should remain in this house and nobody should remove them.'

Milada Müllerová sent letters.

To the president of the republic, Antonín Novotný, for instance. She wrote to him that she had no idea that after the establishment of a socialist state one would have to pay tax on every valuable object. She thought her husband had done that, but didn't go into the details. She begged the president for mercy (she underlined that word), and to allow her collection of paintings by the Czech masters to stay in its place. She was afraid they would end up in antique shops instead of being preserved as an integral collection and made accessible to the public at her villa. She stressed that the woman making this appeal to the president was a sick person, without health insurance, not even a pension.

Ending her letter, she wrote: 'With gratitude, Your Milada Müllerová.'

Part of another letter has survived too, in which she offered the authorities the ultimate argument against the gradual destruction of the villa: 'Adolf Loos' villa has now been nationalized, so any damage done to it is harm inflicted on the nation.'

Underneath, she added: 'Here's to Peace! Milada Müllerová.' But her words made no impression on the authorities.

(The 'fake cousin' has read my book and recognizes me as a serious author, but she thinks it's pointless for me to travel to the north of Italy. She'll be in Prague soon, she'll be visiting her family. It'll be simpler to meet up there.

She tells me when she's going to be in Prague. I'm on the point of leaving Warsaw, and just want to fix an exact place and date for our meeting, so I call her; unfortunately, she has awful flu, and is not coming. Maybe in a while.

Two weeks later she lets me know that she is in Prague now.

But I'm back in Warsaw! All right, I'll buy an air ticket and the day after tomorrow we can meet.

Unfortunately, the day after tomorrow she's going back to Italy.

Then how about meeting in Italy?

She's sometimes in Milan.

Oh, so am I! When will you be there? I'll come.

It's hard to say...

Some time later I call to say I'll be travelling through Milan.

Unfortunately, she has no one to house-sit...)

It's still 2009.

Mrs Čechová's aunt worked at the Villa Müller while the owner was still alive. Mrs Čechová lives nearby and is 'overjoyed that at last I can have a chat about Mrs Müllerová'.

'She was our model! The perfect model of a lady,' she says, over lunch.

'In what sense?'

'"Don't forget", she told me, "a woman should never put on a dark dress after the age of fifty." I remember her in those light, tailor-made suits. She was a very sophisticated lady. We knew the owners of the villas in the neighbourhood. Whenever the little girls said "good day" to one of the grand women who lived here, she wouldn't respond until she'd found out if their daddy was a lawyer. Of all the ladies in the neighbourhood, Mrs Müllerová was the most natural, and she never let it show that she was a better person.'

'I've heard that she still dressed in clothes from before the war.'

'I'm glad you've raised that matter. She didn't dress in old things out of stinginess, as some people claimed. It was her way of declaring, "I refuse to abandon my old life!" She had problems with her blood pressure, she was sickly, but she always pinned her plait of hair in a chic little bun. Towards the end of her life nothing gave her joy anymore. But she was still elegant.'

'How did your aunt come to work at the villa?'

'At our house, we had a drying room and a mangle, but the communists turned it into a living space for the working class. We wanted my aunt from Prostějov in Moravia to live there – she had moved to Prague with her mother. But we couldn't get her registered, for neither love nor money. There were already a few communists living in Ořechovka and neighbouring Střešovice. And they were the kind who weren't unfair to people. We managed to arrange with them for my aunt to be taken on at the Villa Müller as a caretaker and stoker. That got her an employment stamp in Prague and a registration certificate. She was to light the fire in the boiler room, and Mrs Müllerová was officially appointed as the cleaner.'

'So it's not a rumour? Mrs Müllerová was the cleaner in her own villa?'

'Of course not... my aunt cleaned for her. Their friendship grew out of life's misery. My aunt didn't slave away there for long. She was given some eiderdowns as a gift. Mrs Müllerová was very generous. She gave me a metal vase from Asia – where have I put it? For instance, I wanted to pay her for this lamp and this cupboard. She wouldn't have taken a penny, so I lied that a friend of mine was looking for something just like it, and that way she let me pay for them.'

'And did another lady live there with her? A cousin, for instance?'

'For several years. She was very young. I don't want to create a negative impression, but that girl was always taking things out of the villa.'

'What?'

'It's simple. So the communists wouldn't take them away from Mrs Müllerová.'

(I give up on the 'fake cousin'. There's a right time for everything in life. That could be my refrain.

Three years go by. It's 2012.

I'm in Rome to promote the Italian translation of my book, so I call the 'fake cousin' out of the blue and say that from where I am I can easily come to the north of Italy.

You know what, she says, I don't live there anymore. Now I live in the capital. You'd have to come all the way to Rome.

But that's exactly where I am!)

It's May.

We arrange to meet at the Villa Borghese gardens. From afar I see a tall, slender, athletic woman with long black hair. The 'fake cousin' looks a bit too young to have been an art historian while also working for the security service in the 1950s. I ask how she maintains her figure, because I'd like to take care of mine too. She says it's in her genes. She's looked like a model since childhood.

'When I was fifteen, Milada and I were once waiting for the tram when a lady who happened to be passing accosted me to say I had perfect proportions. So for a while I became a model, and I earned quite a lot from it.'

'You were fifteen years old and you already knew Mrs Müllerová?'

'I was thirteen when I went to live with her at the villa.'

'They sent Mrs Müllerová a thirteen-year-old girl?'

'I was surprised myself to be sent there, but I soon felt happy.'

'How did it all start?'

'First, I was expelled from high school. Suddenly, I had no right to study, which in Czechoslovakia was a typical punishment for wayward parents throughout communism.'

'What was the reason?'

'I didn't fully understand, because I was too small. Anyway, in the 1950s it was better not to burden a child with knowledge. I'd overheard that my grandfather had a hotel in Šumava – it's a region that borders Austria – and at our house they found a very detailed map of that area. Espionage! Bad! My other grandfather was a high-school teacher, but he had an artificial fertilizer company, and was also active as a Freemason. A capitalist and a Mason. Bad! Just after the war, my dad's brother was a cultural attaché in Sweden and Finland, and really was the perfect communist. But he knew about someone who'd escaped from Czechoslovakia to Sweden, and didn't report it to the authorities in Prague. Bad! He ended up in solitary confinement. Those were just coincidences – none of them belonged to any mainstream opposition. Dad worked at the ministry of trade, where he set the prices for goods. He got very bored working them out. Maybe the authorities were trying to warn him? Or to keep him in check? I have no idea. At any rate, I found out that I couldn't go to school. What could my parents have done at the time? Nothing. They had to obey the authorities.'

'And you were given the task of going to live in the former millionairess's villa.'

'I was very pleased with this task, because I didn't have to be at home anymore. I had my mission, my world.'

'What exactly was your mission?'

'Auntie – that's what I always called her—'

'Yes, I know.'

'She lived in the villa like in a labour camp. She'd suddenly been left without her furniture, on top of which she had to pay rent. In her own home! Loos' exquisite design became a prison for her. She'd broken her leg at the hip and couldn't get up and down the stairs. She broke it twice! That's the sort of break that can't be put in plaster. It has to heal of its own accord. Her leg was just dangling. It's lucky I was there with her. She had a bathroom upstairs, but how could she reach it? So she slept in the bathroom, because there was a lavatory in there. Luckily it was a large room, so there was enough space for a small couch...'

'And where did you sleep?

'On a couch in the boudoir, and when Milada got better, she slept on it, and I slept on a sofa, under that "railway" window overlooking the salon. She had the whole of that little boudoir barricaded with objects. There was just a narrow corridor between them so she could get through to her bed. You had to watch out for the Chinese vases... We could look down from the window and see the publishers at work, but we didn't really want to; it was a nasty sight. The villa had been designed for young people, with all those steps and landings. Milada couldn't walk anymore, but she was being asphyxiated by her own home, so to speak... There's something I must tell you...'

'I'm eager to hear it...'

'In the boudoir, on the lower level, under the window, there was an exquisite ladies' writing desk, eighteenth century, with two little drawers, so refined... And do you know how talented Adolf Loos was? He fitted a panel onto the wall beneath the window, to make the antique desk look like a museum exhibit against it...'

'And...?'

'Well, it was a brilliant idea for introducing an antique into a modern interior.'

'I thought you were going to tell me something different...'

'I'm just about to! The inside of that house was badly torn apart. I was a girl at the time, I didn't understand art, but I could tell a crime was being committed against something beautiful. When the publishing house was there – later on, when they made it into a Centre for Marxism–Leninism, I'd already emigrated – they divided the rooms with imitation wood panels. It was enough to make you weep. In fact, as soon as the spring came, those editors didn't do much work. They spent most of their time sunbathing on the terraces. They used to steal the newspapers! Milada didn't have a television set or a radio, but she did subscribe to the newspapers. She read them carefully every day. But the awful man who ran the publishing house used to arrive early and pull her newspapers out of the letter box. We complained loud and clear! But he said it wasn't true. So one day I got up before he arrived at work, and I put a month-old newspaper in the letter box, but neatly folded, like new. I went to see him, and there on his desk was the old newspaper, not yet opened. I forced him to confess.'

'For a teenager, you had your ways and means!'

'Oh, I'll tell you about another idea of mine. We had cats. Those people from the publishing house kept screaming and shouting that the cats were doing their business in their rooms. Which was a lie. They staged a production, if I can put it like that, and said to us: "Here's a cat mess!" "All right," I said, "I'll clean it up." I saved the cat mess. "Auntie," I said, "I've got a plan!" Milada could walk then, so we took it to the vet's. We got them to analyse the excrement in their lab and it turned out to be dog mess. The vet officially certified that for us. And that was the end of the accusations.* You know what, we were always having to defend ourselves. The poor thing, she dreamed endlessly about it becoming a museum, she even invited some architecture experts from Vienna. Those people from the publishing house downright hated her.'

'Did they know who you really were?'

---

* In the archive, there's a letter from Milada Müllerová to the management of the pedagogical publishing house, but about marks left by a dog (there are no extant documents about a cat): 'Before seven o'clock this morning your employee, Mr Racek, demanded entry to my bedroom. He would not stop yelling and banging his fists on the door, and when my cousin opened it, he barged into the room. When he demanded that we must instantly remove a stain the dog had left outside the bathroom door, my cousin calmly replied that she would clean the floor at once. Despite which Mr Racek went on yelling and even resorted to violence, hitting my cousin on the neck with a swift blow, and would not let us close the door to the bedroom, although I was still not dressed.'

'Oh yes. Working and living with Milada in that house meant being isolated from the outside world. I had nothing to do with young people. For several years I had no contact with my contemporaries. Her daughter Eva had disappeared, and Milada didn't like her husband. Anyway, he was an unpleasant man. Eva came over from London twice, but she behaved oddly, she wasn't at all interested, in either people or things. She seemed strangely absent. As if she simply couldn't take in what had happened to the house, and how her mother felt about it. Later, she ended up in a mental hospital, and it all became clear.'

'And how did Mrs Müllerová die?'

'I wasn't there then, but I do know. Let's start from the fact that I never saw her show fear. She was afraid of no one and nothing. Of course I don't know how she took her husband's death... Do you know that he died of a heart attack in his study? He wasn't poisoned in the boiler room. He had a stammer... Franz was funny, with that stammer of his. Milada said that he fell out of his pram as a small child, and from then on he stammered.'

'Let's go back to her fear.'

'She was afraid twice, and that second time – I'm convinced – was the cause of her death. She was afraid of the Soviets. When they liberated Prague in 1945, for some time they billeted forty, maybe fifty soldiers on the Müllers. She said they behaved atrociously. There was a low sink in the kitchen for cleaning vegetables, where the waste was washed away. And the Russkies used to go there to piss, and worse. They slept in their boots and got drunk. A nightmare. And when the Soviets invaded Prague again in 1968, eighteen days later Milada had a heart attack from fear. Do you know that she never succeeded in meeting her grandson? That's why she regarded me as a daughter. She loved me... And what beautiful clothes she had... Did I tell you how she used to powder her nose?'

'I have no idea.'

'Through her veil! Through the veil attached to her hat – she never went out without a hat. And we used to go to concerts and exhibitions together. Thanks to her I became interested in finding a profession related to art. In fact, the first time Milada broke her leg was at a concert hall. But she didn't wear her veil only to concerts, she always went into the city like that! Into the communist city, where there was the world's biggest monument to Stalin! She never lost her refined manners. Did you know that she used to have two baths a day?'

'I didn't know that sort of detail.'

'I'm the right person to come to for the details. My parents were very envious of Milada...'

'But they must have had to agree to your mission at the villa?'

'It was their idea in the first place for me to go and live with Auntie, seeing I wasn't allowed to study. Because she was a woman of the world, well read, and she would instil principles in me. Besides, they knew Milada couldn't manage after breaking her leg.'

'It was your parents' idea?'

'Yes, they were very fond of her. In 1962, when I was twenty, I got married, and in 1966 I emigrated. In 1963, when the political climate relaxed, they allowed me to complete school as an extramural student and I was able to graduate from school before emigrating.'

'Very good, but what about the security service...?'

'I had to deal with them twice. Once, they came to search the villa – I don't know what they were looking for, but earlier they'd sent the Müllers' former maid to do some spying. She admitted that she was there to check that certain paintings hadn't been sold on the quiet. And you know what, whenever Milada sold one of the pictures, I signed a statement to say I'd got it from her for looking after her, as a relative. The second time I had dealings with the secret police was when I came to Prague for a visit. It was the 1970s. A man invited me to a café for a chat, and he said that as I was living in Germany and had a German husband, the fatherland needed my help. When I got back to Munich, the German secret police immediately invited me for a chat to say they knew about the Czechoslovak proposal and advised me not to cooperate. That's as much as I had to do with any of them.'

'But as a thirteen-year-old...'

'What "as a thirteen-year-old"?'

'Oh, nothing...'

(Twice, at intervals, I checked whether Jitka Klinkenberger, née Helfertová, had cooperated with the Czechoslovak secret police. The ministry of internal affairs archive, and then the

Czech Institute of National Remembrance, informed me that no such employee, collaborator or agent had ever existed.

Then I hired a Czech detective agency that specialized in investigating the past of particular individuals. 'There is no evidence of cooperation, and we are one hundred per cent sure that this lady has no past as an agent,' they replied after I'd made the bank transfer.

I hereby ask Ms Klinkenberger's forgiveness for revealing this only here and now, but I wanted to convey my amazement during our conversation and to sustain the reader's curiosity.)

After the collapse of communism the Villa Müller was restored to the Müllers' daughter, Eva Materna, within the general restitution of property that took place in the Czech Republic. Suddenly, it became an object of interest for several wealthy Czechs. However, Mrs Materna sold it to the city for the standard price, despite being offered twice as much by private individuals.* In 1995 a team of art historians, architects and craftsmen began to renovate the house, and restored it to its almost perfect prewar condition.

For instance, an art museum in Tokyo was asked to find a lantern similar to the one with the autumn flower pattern that had disappeared from the summer dining room.

---

* I wrote to George Materna, Mr and Mrs Müller's grandson, at his London address. His mother, Eva, is no longer alive. He replied that he knows nothing about the villa except for what he has read in newspaper articles. I promised him I'd reconstruct his grandmother's life story.

Someone had stolen the collection of porcelain from the study, or perhaps Mrs Müllerová had sold it. The present one is on loan from the Museum of the City of Prague.

The porcelain washbasin with its attractive curves and ovals made by the English firm Twyford's, which stood in the lavatory next to the cloakroom, was so badly damaged that it wasn't fit for restoration. Unfortunately, Twyford's was no longer able to reproduce it, so the basin was sculpted anew by a famous Czech potter.

Only one of the Chippendale chairs had survived with its original fabric intact, but, using it as a model, new material was woven to upholster the remaining seventeen.

The bidet had been torn out of the bathroom, but a suitable one was found in another house of a similar age to the Villa Müller. The original sanitary fittings and sewage pipes did not work anymore, and the bathroom was unusable. 'There's no blood flowing through the veins of the house' – that was one of the saddest comments I heard about the villa.

The villa has become its own museum.

An architect tracked down the Müllers' daughter to record an interview with her. The old lady sat down at the microphone and began to insist that she was five years old, and that she was the little girl who lived in the villa.

THE BOMB
OF TIME EXPLODES

Once it was in dismal surroundings. The house it was in was a wreck, and it was like a junk room in an attic no one had visited for years. On either side of the entrance the plaster was falling off the façade.

Now the street looks bright, the house has been repainted, and it has been tidied up. All the objects have been sorted out, put into groups and dusted.

The old Christmas tree baubles have changed place, from a middle to a bottom shelf. Eighteen months ago there were seventeen of them: twelve red, two gold, two silver and one blue. They're still lying in a small square wicker basket. Not a single one has gone.

Twelve used ladies' hats, felt, fur and wool, ranging from white to dark brown – as if straight off the heads of women who have reached their eighties – have moved from the back of a middle shelf to a shelf by the window. Although they're on view, and the sun has spent a long time disinfecting them with its rays, none of them has found a new wearer.

Five ancient clothes brushes with dark wooden handles and stiff black bristles have been transferred from one wall to another, but are still keeping each other company. One of them still has a silvery fibre stuck to it, possibly a hair, just as it did two years ago.

The countless empty picture frames are still countless, but now they've been freed from chaos and are lined up in size order. Like everything in here, they're standing on plain shelves made of raw wood.

Six months ago, the general despondency was disrupted by the white plaster figure of a kissing couple – a semi-naked woman with long hair and a semi-naked man who, instead of embracing the girl with both arms, had his left hand on his own hip. Maybe the artist wanted to emphasize his triceps, biceps and beautifully carved pecs? The plaster figure, the only item to bring joy in here, has gone.

Unfortunately, nothing else catches my attention that could now disturb the prevailing gloom. Anything that doesn't yield to it is doomed to a short-term stay here. Every more joyful item soon leaves the place.

THE DEAD PEOPLE'S SHOP

at 9, Döbrentei Street in Budapest is open every day, including Sundays.

Its name includes the phrase 'flea market'. The customer expects to buy 'antiques' or 'bric-a-brac', but not things left behind by the dead. We want to blur the truth, because it's easier to say and think 'I bought an antique' or 'I bought an old trinket' than 'I bought some evidence of death.' It's probably just to do with wanting to stay in a good mood, but perhaps there's more to it. Maybe it's to do with what is for ever our favourite occupation – something that may in fact be vital to human life: putting off the thought of NOT THERE.

And yet any object that's over a certain age must have belonged to someone who's not alive anymore. There's no other possibility, and no words can obscure this truth. Before the bomb of time exploded, the object filled someone's space, and once it had completed its mission, if it was lucky, it ended up with someone else; if it was less lucky, it ended up here. And with no luck at all it went in the dustbin. Joseph Brodsky described the bomb of time in his essay 'In a Room and a Half', which is about his parents. Their bodies, clothes, telephone, keys and furniture had gone and would never be recovered, just as if a bomb had fallen on their room and a half (that was the share of a communal Leningrad apartment that they occupied). Not a neutron bomb, because it would have left the furniture intact, but a bomb of time, which even destroys memory. 'The building still stands, but the place is wiped out clean and new tenants, no, troops move in to occupy it.'* So I imagine that here, on the Buda side of the city, on the banks of the Danube, everything that has survived the explosion of a bomb of time has accumulated.

---

* Joseph Brodsky, *Less Than One: Selected Essays*, Farrar, Straus & Giroux, 1986.

And so I insist that the purpose of this shop is to gather evidence of death, and it is carrying out this task extremely well.

The owner, Zsolt Rédei, often goes to dead people's houses. The families invite him to come and choose whatever he wants.

One night in 2004 he was walking through Montmartre, in Paris. Suddenly, he noticed a house with an open front door and a winding staircase beyond it. On the walls in the stairwell there were some small pictures, plates and items whose purpose he couldn't make out in the dark. He went up the stairs into a room crammed with furniture and objects from various periods, ranging from the 1920s to the 1960s. (He was an estate agent, so he knew something about styles of furniture.) And there at a table sat three elderly gentlemen, drinking wine.

They were surrounded by a clutter of old chairs, wardrobes and cabinets... all filled with glasses, china and tablecloths. He thought he must have entered a private flat, so he apologized, but the gentlemen explained that it was a shop. One of them was a retired doctor who had inherited a bachelor flat from his grandmother. He and his retired friends had formed a company, opened this place, and now spent most of their time here. They treated the Hungarian to a glass of red wine while he chose an object costing five euros. He left with something more valuable as well: the decision to give up his job in property sales in fifteen years' time, and to open a similar shop at home.

The rule at Zsolt Rédei's place is this: the items cost one, two, five or ten euros.

Outside the entrance there's an old bike with a dummy's head wearing a hat and pince-nez attached to the basket, and hanging from the handlebars there's a worn-out leather valise with a Malév sticker – Malév was the Hungarian airline that was also killed by a bomb of time when it went bust after existing for sixty-six years.

There's always a large black dog called Maci lying on the floor by the entrance, so you have to step over him.

This is my favourite shop in Budapest, and possibly in the whole world. I visit it twice a year. Whenever I go back to my hotel from there or, like today, to my rented flat at 4/17 Ferenciek Square, I always wash my hands thoroughly. It's not that they might be dirty, it's more of a psychological issue. Now, as I've been writing about the place, I've used the washbasin twice. The mere topic is responsible for that: I have a physical feeling of my hands being coated in a thin but invisible layer of dirt.

But that is no obstacle to my fondness for the shop.

So here, twice a year, I buy objects left behind by dead people. There are other individuals who like to spend their time rummaging in here too. We don't want to buy things online. We want to look at them, touch them and fall in love with them.

Does a picture in an old gilded frame on our desk mean one thing if we remember that it once belonged to someone who's dead now, and another thing if we pretend it never belonged to anyone? Yes.

In the first case, we form a metaphysical relationship with the previous owner. They too held the picture in their hand, they too wiped the glass. They shifted it a few inches this way or that on their desk. Simply knowing that someone enjoyed its existence in the past, and might have been pleased that someone else is still enjoying it, makes me happy, and gives my life another little bit of meaning. I hope I represent a first-rate stage in the object's existence.

I am convinced that being aware of the death of the former owner can help us to find the right proportions in life. If I know that I'm not immortal, I'll live life in a different way.

(Hanna Krall has just written to tell me to be careful not to set my golden thoughts in stone too easily. And that if I must express them, I should do it with doubt, reflection, a question mark, helplessly, and as if asking for advice.)

If I know that I'm not immortal, will I live life in a different way? It has also occurred to me that our death brings relief to objects too.

Does our death bring relief to objects too?

(I don't know which is better.)

In one of Věra Linhartová's *Stories about Whatever*, the wife of a mime artist who practises at home has decided to tidy up their cluttered apartment so that her husband won't trip over any obstacles. 'What if we have to leave here?' she asks, and starts giving away old clothes and burning books, photos and letters.*

'Yet, once removed, the things returned in the regret that she felt immediately upon their removal, and because she lost track of what she had got rid of and what still remained, the flat had filled with all the things that had ever been inside it, and this lasting presence of theirs was even more oppressive than ever before.' We can agree that the objects in Döbrentei Street don't carry a burden – they no longer return to anyone in the form of regret.

---

* A reminder that Věra Linhartová (born 1938) paralysed Viola Fischerová to such an extent that for decades she hadn't the courage to write. Linhartová herself stopped writing poetry and stories in Czech fifty years ago, when her language 'ran out'. She claims she wrung so much out of it that there was nothing left, and as a result she loathes her old books and never looks at them, even though the Czechs keep reissuing them. As a result of her lack of interest, the mistakes that appeared in the first edition keep being reprinted. For her, the Czech language is over and done with. She always wanted to be a Parisian and to write in French, which is what happened. So she has no reason – she says – to return to the Czech Republic, literally or symbolically. She adds that a writer doesn't have to be a prisoner of their own language. She lives in Paris, where for many years she worked at the Guimet Museum, which is the national museum of Asian art, and wrote specialist books on Japanese painting. Let's return briefly to the chapter entitled 'Reading Walls': so we could say that because of Linhartová, Fischerová didn't write until 1984, and because of the limitations of the Czech language, Linhartová has not written in it since 1968, which gives them sixteen years of parallel silence. When, in Milan Kundera's book of essays, *Encounter*, I read V.L.'s statement that a writer cannot be a prisoner of their own language, I very much wanted to talk to her about this NOT THERE. Unfortunately, she doesn't give interviews. For admirers of her fiction her NOT THERE is consistent and perhaps indisputable.

But can we be sure? What if one of their owners is still alive, and relinquished the object to make money?

To make two or three euros? No way.

So their owners have to be dead.

As we can see, the things that accumulate in the dead people's shop have an obscure history. It is a blank space for the customer. I may be committing a semantic crime, but it occurred to me that each of these objects is 'a thing in itself'. This has to do with the *noumenon* that Immanuel Kant wrote about. A thing in itself, he claimed, is unknowable and exists beyond the scope of our minds. It is transcendental, we do not and cannot know anything about it, because we lack the relevant tools. So 'a thing in itself' cannot become 'a thing for us'.

What for Kant is transcendental, in the dead people's shop we can ascribe to specific physical objects. The things, like missives from the past sent by strangers to whom we shall never speak, give us nothing but themselves.

Maybe that's better?

Maybe this is the only way they can be, or are, a pure message? Ready to be interpreted like a poem? You don't have to know a poet to interpret their verses.

Drawers full of private photographs. Thousands of homeless photos given away wholesale. The life in these pictures is not gracing anyone's life at all. It isn't bringing joy to the descendants of the people posing in them. As we're in Budapest, and

I happen to be reading an excellent novel about a submissive man whom the air of this city carries along, just as water carries plankton, I shall quote the main character, who has quite incisively recognized this phenomenon: 'If I may be so bold as to make a rather grand statement, taking photos could be said to be a way of informing the models that they're on the road to oblivion.'

Yet I did not see the moment coming when András, the main character in Krzysztof Varga's novel *Sonnenberg*, would have himself photographed, even less take selfies. And a good thing too, because our selfies will disappear during the next great magnetic storm and won't be as lucky as the photographs on Döbrentei Street, which exist on paper.

Who buys photographs of someone else's life? I know from the owners of an art gallery that photographic portraits are the hardest thing to sell. You have to be very open emotionally to introduce a stranger's face into your home, especially a close-up. A picture of a favourite writer or actor is of someone we know and admire, so we feel as if they're close to us, they're part of the family. But what about an unfamiliar face? In your intimate environment? It won't find many takers. And who would want to be the owner of an album containing forty-nine wedding photos featuring a couple they've never met, taken in the early 1950s? Or their wedding portrait?

Zsolt Rédei explained it to me: 'Just imagine, there are young people from western Europe or the USA who come into my shop. They were born outside the communist world, and they don't know anything about life in our countries. So they buy this sort of photograph, or authentic artefacts from old eastern Europe. They're fascinated by every detail in them. I must admit that the main item I collect from dead people's houses is photographs.'

Twice a year, I buy gifts for my friends at the dead people's shop. I give these objects up for adoption. I tell them I've brought them something from somebody else's life, though to be precise I should say from somebody else's non-life.

I too have adopted a small picture from there. It's in a copper-coloured wooden frame.

It was emotion at first sight.

It shows a young man whose dark hair is neatly parted. We view him in profile. He has prominent cheekbones and clearly defined eyebrows. He's wearing a jacket and a white shirt. He is probably kneeling (we don't know, because he's only visible from the waist up) before a figure of Jesus on the cross. That we don't entirely know either, because all we can see are the overlapping feet and the legs below the knees. The man is kissing the left foot, and his hands are holding on to the cross.

Behind the man several candles are burning. Their dim light fades against a blurred sepia background. The picture – as the caption tells us – was taken in 1933, a meaningful year for me, because my dad was born in it. The print was issued by the St Anthony's Guild, based in Paterson, New Jersey. The guild had its own printing firm, apparently the biggest in the United

States at the time. It is estimated to have published millions of similar pictures, which were designed to encourage young men to enter the priesthood.

The model who posed for them was Thomas F. Lynch.

Under the drawing there's a message: 'MAY THY WAY BE MY WAY.'

Except that in the picture Jesus' legs look like female legs. They're smooth and shapely. The feet haven't been pierced by a nail.

Nor is it an ordinary kiss – you can see the passion in it.

Didn't the artist know how to draw realistic-looking male legs? Bonier than that?

Or maybe there's a hidden message?

Jesus will be your substitute for a woman? Your Jesus will be everything for you? Including your love object?

I found another drawing on the internet in which the same model is raising his head to look a naked Jesus in the eyes. It's not an ordinary look, not surprisingly, because who would look at Jesus in an ordinary way? But the look in the eyes of Thomas F. Lynch, who embodies the image of the model Catholic, is quite unsettling. He's looking at Jesus with pure lust.

The creator of these pictures was Charles Bosseron Chambers (1882–1964), known as the Catholic Norman Rockwell, who was a major figure in American art. As we know, harnessing talent to serve an ideology is the best way to kill it, so Chambers' works are mawkish and mannered, and the only quality we can see in them is decent craftsmanship. The critics did not spare the artist. So perhaps, knowing that the saccharine tone of his drawings was an indelible feature, Chambers wanted to infuse them with at least a touch of eroticism? Hordes of committed American Catholics ('The American mindset is quite banal' – was it Andy Warhol who said that?) accepted his visions without batting an eyelid.

Thomas F. Lynch, who was Chambers' regular model, came from an Irish family that had produced eleven children. Only six of them survived. Thomas did not become a priest – he became a doctor – though two of his brothers did. A third began his studies at the seminary but soon abandoned them when he realized he wasn't a good enough orator. A fourth brother, the oldest, was a qualified smith who worked on the maintenance of the Statue of Liberty, and also produced halberd blades for Hollywood films. Thomas had lots of children too, two daughters and five sons. His son Greg remembers him as a handsome, honest man, always in a suit, and always hurrying off to help the needy. Greg only had fleeting thoughts of donning a cassock. His real desire was to become a policeman. Unfortunately, in 1971 he had a motorbike accident and lost his left leg, as well as his dream of serving in the police force. He became an acclaimed specialist in fitting artificial limbs. Greg's wife, Michelle, attended a Catholic high school. On the wall next to the administrative office there was a reproduction of one of Chambers' pictures for which Thomas Lynch had posed. 'I walked past it hundreds of times without knowing that one day I'd marry the model's son,' she said. Greg's children...

I could go on with the story of the Lynch family, but... (When I'm silent I feel as if I'm not there.)

The day before yesterday I placed the picture of Thomas F. Lynch kissing Jesus' feminine feet on my temporary desk in Budapest. And at once I feel good, I feel at home. I don't have to have my favourite photograph in front of me, which I didn't bring with me from Warsaw anyway. I don't even have to be sitting at my usual desk. An adopted object is capable of filling the temporary NOT THERE for me.

'And who's interested in other people's letters and postcards?' I asked Zsolt.

'There are people,' he replied, 'plenty of them, who find pleasure in reading old personal correspondence. Because it's intriguing, for instance, that in the mid-twentieth century a country lawyer was courting a girl who was studying law in Budapest...'

Sent once. Also read by someone once, maybe twice or three times.

Between the picture postcard and the letter there was an intermediate form: the plain postcard. The picture postcard has a photograph on one side (a landscape, castle, marketplace, etc.), whereas the plain postcard has its message on view like the picture postcard, but there is no picture on it. I have a theory that plain postcards were sent by people who didn't want to write a letter, which demanded a longer message, but didn't want to send a picture postcard either, because of its association with greetings and an air of frivolity. This format allowed the sender to be concise, and justified a short message ('I've run out of space'), but without depriving them of the gravity that a picture postcard would take away.

Of course, it's also worth remembering that the cost of postage for postcards has always been cheaper than for letters.

At Döbrentei Street, the plain postcards are kept in a wicker egg basket. The oldest one I found in there was dated 1923, the most recent 1992. I decided to take one of them away with me for ever. Perhaps I was gripped by what Marek Bieńczyk, writing about Baudelaire, called 'a maniacal need for an idea'. So I picked up the basket by its large thin handle, stood up straight, took a deep breath and exhaled, as there was a thirty-degree heatwave in the city, and picked one at random!

A postcard, abandoned by the sender and the addressee for ever.

It was sent on 12 December 1965 from Dunakeszi, a suburb of Budapest, to the city centre. It is addressed to Zsolt Domboy, and the sender signs his name as Janos H.

Dear Ildi and Zsolt,

For the past two weeks I've been battling the flu. There was one day when I felt all right, but most of the time I've been very ill. I think the Devil's waiting for my skin. (It wouldn't be too sorry by now.) I hoped I wouldn't feel so bad today, and that at least I'd be able to make a show of it. But this evening I felt so ill again that I can't go anywhere, or get anything started. The worst of it is that I'm terribly weak, and if it goes on bothering me for another week I'm not sure I'll ever get rid of it. I'm sorry I failed to think of everything. It's only coming to mind now, and I'm doing my best to make up for the backlog. I wrote to Koczag, he wrote back, and just imagine, he wished me Merry Christmas. As soon as I'm better I'll be in touch.

Love from Janos

So, here in this book, we've saved one postcard, perhaps more than just that.

APPROPRIATION

I've become a photographer, like everyone who comes to New York, I guess.

I'm appropriating images, like everyone who comes to New York, I guess.

Photo 1: a blonde man, almost naked, tanned. His hair is escaping from under a cowboy hat. Seen from behind, in Times Square. He turns his head towards the photographer, he has a flirtatious look and protruding buttocks. His white briefs sport the message: NAKED COWBOY.

Photo 2: an African American in a black woollen cap is standing among the passers-by with a sign that says: 'Google It!!! Jesus Christ Is GOD'. The man looks appreciatively at the photographer.

Photo 3: on the edge of a kerb, between a bin and a car wheel, there are twelve bald women's heads made of plastic. The site: Forty-Second Street, between Fifth and Sixth.

Photo 4: a large group of people of every skin colour. They're leaning forward with their legs astride. They're holding out their hands as if each were carrying an invisible object. In the background there's a skyscraper, a tree and a street sign: 'West 42nd Street'. All thirty-two faces of the people exercising are focused, fixed on the man dictating their movements.

Photo 5: beyond a window with black-and-white drapes, within hand's reach, there's a grey brick wall. It's an awful sight, the window is pretty much walled-in, but it could be a reason to be cheerful: it's an archetypal window! A window with a view of a brick wall – but it's in New York! Daylight trickles through the thin gap between roofs, so that you can see the mortar between the bricks. Like cream oozing from between the layers of a squashed cake. The location: a hotel room on Forty-Fifth Street.

Photo 6: a small, tubby, fair-haired man in a peaked cap and a tracksuit top is standing in front of park railings. He's smiling into the camera – two seconds ago, he agreed to have his picture taken. He's holding a pink card with the message: TOO SHY TO TALK TO HOT GIRLS.

Photo 7: long steel columns in a single bunch. They're bent, like a wilted bouquet of wild grass. Coated in rust. This is part of the North Tower façade between the ninety-first and ninety-ninth floors. Now the twisted scrap metal stands like a sculpture in a gallery. (Reality has dethroned art, but that's another story.) The photographer had to kneel down to immortalize such a tall object in its entirety. To allow him to take a 'clean' picture of it, the museum guard considerately moved a few steps away.

Photo 8: on a rack there are coat hangers with tops thickly sprinkled with cream-coloured dust. The photographer cannot tear his eyes from it: how has that dust from the rubble remained on the fabric for fifteen years? The dust-coated interior of the Chelsea Jeans store within the Ground Zero zone has been enclosed in a glass fish tank.

Photo 9, if it could be taken: a ladies' black leather handbag with a metal handle, broken and puckered like pasta ribbons. Concrete or some other hard material has cut through the metal and the leather. Behind the handbag hangs the portrait of a woman in a white hat who looks exactly like Linda Evans as Krystle in *Dynasty*.

The caption next to the picture says: 'Purse belonging to Catherine Patricia Salter (Assistant Vice President, Aon Corporation, South Tower, 92nd floor). Referred to as a "super aunt" by her eleven nieces and nephews, Catherine Salter remained close to family and friends in her native Ohio despite her transfer in 2000 from a local Aon Corporation office to the firm's New York City branch. Her fondness for shopping, especially for designer pocketbooks, was noticeable to family and friends as well as to clients she met as assistant vice president. Recovered from the debris of Ground Zero, this clutch purse was returned to Catherine's mother by the NYPD's Property Recovery Unit.'

The picture would look like that if the uniformed guard had not started saying in a raised voice: 'No photo, please! No photo, please!'

In a country where 'everything is on show and 'everything is for sale', at the 9/11 Memorial and Museum there's a display case that you're not allowed to photograph. Gathered in it are personal items found in the ruins of the World Trade Center. They are exhibited alongside photographs of their lost owners. The picture of Catherine Patricia Salter and her handbag are the first things you see. Further on there are phones, shoes, wallets, notebooks, faces young and old...

We have the right to appropriate many images, but not these objects and not these faces.

He came into the funeral parlour.

'I'd like to order the cheapest burial,' he said.

'The cheapest?' the employee asked.

'Yes, he was a very bad man.'

'The cheapest would be without dressing the deceased,' she suggested. 'The body could be wrapped in a shroud, for instance.'

He asked her to specify what exactly a shroud was, because in the pictures in church it looked like serious fabric.

'It can be an ordinary sheet,' she explained.

'I can spare that man one sheet,' he said, relieved, and moved on to the main point. 'Can this person have no grave at all?'

'None at all?' she asked again.

'None at all. I don't want to put him in a grave. I just want nothing to be left of him. No trace.'

'It's possible, but even the ashes in an urn – which I'm sure you'll agree is a slightly smaller trace than a body in a coffin – have to be put somewhere. In a columbarium, for instance.'

'What if I tip the ashes into a dustbin?'

'The law doesn't allow that, though there is a small loophole in it,' she added.

He suspects that he merited the undertaker's friendly attitude by stroking her dog as soon as he came in, smacking his lips and praising its charms.

'The loophole allows you to declare that the deceased will be buried not in Warsaw but in Płock, for example. You'll take the urn, and no one will check if it ever reached Płock.'

He scattered the bad man in several places: on a riverbank in the village where the bad man was born, some on the road, and some in the woods. 'Look here,' he said in a low tone, 'I've given you a shroud, plus fourteen zlotys for a bus ticket, and I've united you with nature. And that'll have to do for you.'

He threw the urn in the rubbish bin. He got back to his apartment in the city centre. From the table he picked up the bottle of vodka, the single shot glass and the doily on which the urn had stood all night. He glanced around the flat, which he'd recently had rebuilt. Formerly, there had been three interconnected rooms: the bad man had had the room at one end, the mother had the room at the other end, and he and his sister had the room in the middle. A very uncomfortable position. Sometimes the bad man stopped in the middle room and made a speech. He never raised his hand to his son or his daughter. Instead of his trouser belt he used words.

When, at the oncology ward, they asked him to bring in the deceased's ID card, he started looking through his papers and came to the feeble conclusion that the bad man had started drinking because he was counting on becoming First Secretary, but hadn't succeeded. And then the world of first and last secretaries had evaporated for ever. (Let's get it straight: maybe not for ever.)

'I wonder if your father is somewhere,' I think aloud.

'You know what,' he says, on a warm summer evening, over a bottle of white wine on a long balcony in the city centre, where he grows tomatoes, peppers and herbs, 'you know, I stopped fearing death in the equatorial rainforest. It's the oldest forest in the world, millions of years old, because it has always grown closest to the sun and looks down on freezing over. It's home to forest elephants, smaller than the ones on the savannah. But their droppings are ginormous. When I leaned over one of them, I saw all the life it had attracted. Flies, beetles and ants were bustling around it like at a diner. And it occurred to me that we all supply fuel for nature. Our life has its greatest meaning when it provides material for decomposition.'

'What about our consciousness?' I ask. 'What I'm sorriest about losing is consciousness.'

'But plants talk to each other,' he says. 'Did you know that the world is entwined by a huge underground mushroom spawn? It goes in between the roots of plants and it's like a telephone cable. In China they planted some tomatoes in a field, and placed selected plants in glass jars. When aphids came along, they attacked the tomatoes growing at the edge of the plantation, but not the ones in the middle. They produced a toxin on their leaves to fight the aphids. The tomatoes at the edge had sent them a warning of the threat with the help of that mushroom spawn. The tomatoes in the jars didn't get the message, because they were isolated, and they all perished. So communication, and thus consciousness, doesn't die. And so what if it's not information about Schopenhauer? Aphids matter more than Schopenhauer.

'My father? He's there – after all, I scattered a bit of him among the trees in the woods.'

AN EXTREMELY SHORT LECTURE ABOUT ^{NOT THERE} BY HANNA KRALL

'Everything must have its own form, Mariusz, its own rhythm. Especially absence.'

REPORTAGE

Reportage is the inability to survive one's own existential experience with the help of fiction.

THINGS JUST HAPPEN

I

There are two of them.

This isn't the relevant couple yet.

Only one of them is relevant.

This scene is just a prelude to the actual story.

They're sitting in armchairs facing each other. The first one, sitting under the window, can look at the clock to see how much time is left until the end. The second one, sitting nearer the door, can't see the clock, but is wearing a wristwatch, though dares not glance at it to check the time. (A few months later this person will admit this fear, upon which the first one will ask: 'And what do you think about that?')

Now the second person, whom we're going to call 'the man', starts to open his heart: 'It's something I've never told anyone before. Sometimes I feel as if I'm even hiding it from myself...'

'Please go on, I'm listening,' replies the first person, using their ritual response.

'I muddle up the young men who come to see me,' says the man. 'I get their names mixed up, and the faces totally. You know what, I'm incapable of recognizing those boys in the street afterwards. In fact, what matters most is for them to leave as quickly as possible. And that the same boy never comes more than once.

'...'

'Only the towel never changes.'

'The towel?'

'Not the same one, of course. Because I give each boy a new, clean one. Ironed. I can't bear towels that haven't been ironed. But as soon as one of these fellows goes away, leaving the used towel behind, I don't put it in the washing machine or the laundry basket. I use that towel myself. It dries, and then I wipe myself with it.'

'You wipe yourself with it.'

(This is not a question. The first man sometimes repeats what the second man has just said, to be sure that's what he heard.)

'As soon as the boy leaves I touch that towel, I press it to my face. I find that very pleasant, I could calmly fall asleep on it,' explains the man. 'And I only toss the towel in the washing machine once I've used it myself.'

'And what do you think about that?'

2

The man writes: 'Dear sir, unfortunately I must discontinue my psychotherapy. I'd like to thank you very much for your efforts. I realize that o-n-l-y two years will have gone by soon, and the therapy isn't complete, but I'm no longer able to come regularly that early in the morning three times a week. It's beyond my endurance.'

'Perhaps,' the man wonders, 'I should add a nice comment?'

'What I've found most valuable is being opened up by your recurring question, "And what do you think about that?"'

3

The man is with someone much younger than he is. They're walking down the rue Saint-Honoré. The wind ruffles the younger man's dark-brown hair. In sunshine, but also in the light of halogen lamps, there's a cherry-red sheen on that hair.

'Sweetest K,' says the man. 'What the heck, I had to come all the way to Paris with you to realize what happiness is.'

'So what's the new thing you've realized, Little Mole?'

'That I just have to be walking beside you, like now, looking at you, and that's happiness. I swear I need nothing else.'

The younger man's glance and smile could probably be described, but not without a degree of kitsch, so let's not try. Anyway, the younger man would rather they weren't described.

'But I don't know, the man continues, 'if I hadn't gone to psychotherapy ten years ago perhaps it might not have come to us walking along together like this. Without it there'd be a great big void in my life to this day.'

'Little Mole! You can't be afraid of a void!'

'Why not?'

'A void has its value too, just like whatever might fill it.'

Now they're walking along in silence. They've bought shoes: the younger man has a bulky suede pair, and the older man has trainers. As the man adjusts the shoebox in his bag he has no idea he's about to hear the most important words in his life. Things that matter never reveal themselves to him ceremonially. They just show up without warning, in a supermarket checkout queue, or while walking away from a café table after leaving a tip for the waiter.

'Dearest K,' says the man, 'do you know how happy I am that you'll be there to hold my hand when I die? It's the mark of a life fulfilled, if you've got someone to hold…'

'You can knock that out of your head, Little Mole. I won't be there to hold your hand.'

'What do you mean?'

'I won't be here anymore.'

'Where will you be?'

'I won't be anywhere.'

4

The policemen are tired, or possibly fed up. At midnight, they went out onto the balcony to watch the fireworks. To the left, above the roof of a school, the spire of the Palace of Culture is clearly visible. It looks as if it's spraying red, white and blue flames. The policemen are sending texts to say 'Happy New Year.'

They're all waiting for someone more senior to turn up.

A minute after midnight the dead man's phone starts jumping, again and again. On the screen a series of names appears: 'Mama', 'Brother', 'Sister-in-law', 'Dad'. Who's going to answer? The policemen refuse.

These days, the man ('What did I do all night, while he was lying on the floor and those people kept coming and going?') unfortunately cannot give an account of those hours.

It's coming up to five a.m. The prosecutor announces: 'I'm satisfied that it's not suicide and no third parties were involved in the death.'

But the flat has to be sealed.

It's not the man's flat. He can't understand why it has to be sealed if it's neither murder nor suicide, but he does understand that he can't stay there. Indeed, he has no right to do so.

'Mr Prosecutor,' he asks, 'may I take something from here?'

'The rules don't allow it.'

'But I just want a souvenir. From the fridge, that mascot. The little mole from the Czech cartoons.'

'Let's agree that I might not notice,' says the prosecutor.

5

Three months later, early spring.

The man gets an email from a friend; she and her husband have a wooden house on a slope above a river. Ordinarily they live in the Warsaw district of Ursynów, and for years the man has made fun of his friend – who's known as a metaphysical author – for writing her books in a block of flats. She always patiently insists that she does her writing by the river, among the pine trees. Where 'the air is soft, sheets of mist were hovering above the slope this morning, and now I'm sitting on the porch and I'm not wasting my time'. In her email, she reports that today her husband noticed that the blue tulips are starting to sprout. The younger man planted those bulbs, which he brought back from Holland, on 11 November. He did it under the pine trees, where no one plants flowers. He said he'd plant them chaotically and theatrically.

'K has spoken,' says the friend, because to her it's quite normal for blue tulip sprouts to be a form of conversation.

'He doesn't speak to me,' the man writes back. 'He'd already told me everything. Except that I understood nothing.'

The man hadn't understood the gift he gave him – Gogol's *Dead Souls* – a week before he died.

He hadn't understood 'I won't be anywhere.'

He hadn't understood the picture either. The oil painting.

They'd once missed an Auction of Young Art, where the pictures exhibited had a minimum price of five hundred zlotys each. In the auction catalogue, the younger man found a small canvas by a debut artist, but the older man thought it unimpressive. Brown, yellow and grey. The picture was of an escalator, at a shopping mall perhaps. There were human figures riding on it. And above all this it said: 'Things just happen.'

'But Little Mole, that's brilliant!'

'What?'

'Things just happen.'

6

It turned out no one had bid for the picture. The man found the artist* and bought it for the younger man as a present. The younger man hung the picture by the window in his flat.

'How could I have dismissed the comment that "things just happen"?!' he confides in his writer friend in an email, though he knows that not dismissing it would have been worth the same.

'Oh, how I wish it was three years from now already!'

'Three years from now?' asks the friend.

'I want to age and age and age as fast as possible. I don't know anyone who wants to get older quickly, but I do...'

'Get older? Oh my god, why?'

'Because then I'll be further away from the pain. That's why I want it to be three years from now.'

7

Eighteen months on from New Year's Eve, the long May weekend.

The man could deny this incident ever happened, and so defend himself against recurring shame and humiliation. But as he can't do that, let him do the opposite, and talk about it.

The man is walking along Broadway.

---

* The artist was Justyna Janikowska.

For the nth time in his life, but perhaps like many people in the world, for the nth time he can't believe it – is he really walking down Broadway, is he really crossing Fifty-Seventh Street, then Fifty-Sixth... or is this just an American movie?

It's Friday, before midnight, the man has been to see a show at the Metropolitan and is carrying the weekend edition of the *New York Times* under his arm. ('S says would you please bring him the fat Sunday edition of the *New York Times*? It might weigh as much as three kilos but we'll pay you back for the excess baggage – J') That's odd: the Sunday newspaper is on sale at a kiosk at seven p.m. on a Friday. The wonders of America... ('What a pity I can't read or speak English,' the man writes back, 'it's several fat newspapers in one. And what fantastic illustrations!')

The man notices a bar with Italian food that's open round the clock. He goes in and sits at a table in the middle of the room. There's no one apart from the staff and an old couple: a fat wife and a thin husband, that's how he mentally categorizes them. He sits with his back to them.

He has already ordered soup when two young men come into the bar, one in a T-shirt with the letters NYU on it. They sit down by the window, opposite the man, giving him a view of their profiles. The NYU student – as the man categorizes him – is sitting on the right. As he leans forward, the halogen light casts a cherry-red sheen on his brown hair.

The man takes out his iPhone, pretends to be looking through his messages, switches off the sound, and opens the camera. He takes three photos of the boy, imperceptibly. The students are absorbed in conversation. Another three.

The man starts to eat, but stops – 'Let's say the soup is too hot,' he thinks to himself – and checks his messages again...

Then he starts and stops his salad.

'Wait a moment, my darling K, I'll just take one more photo of you...'

'Did I think that, or say it?' he wonders.

After his meal he picks up the iPhone, summons the waiter and asks for the check. Then, from the corner of his eye, he notices the fat woman getting up.

Now, straight in front of him he sees her go up to the young men, lean over them and start to whisper.

His first thought: 'They must know each other. How amazing that even in New York friends can bump into each other.'

But then he sees that both the woman and the students have suddenly turned towards him.

He gets up, puts on his coat, leaves the change for the waiter, and is heading for the exit when he remembers the *New York Times* for S in Warsaw. He goes back for the newspaper left on a chair.

The photographed student gets up too, and bars his way. First the man discovers that there's no cherry-red sheen on his hair. He walks towards him and... fuck... the student says something in English... 'I'm sorry,' he says, definitely, and then, 'iPhone, photo, meee, photo, iPhone, please...' or something of the kind.

The man feels he's about to keel over. He remembers the time he was on stage at the theatre and completely forgot his lines – it all went dark before his eyes then too, but he didn't fall over, he just had to say something, anything.

'Ayam sori, no anderstend,' he replies, trying to give his answer an absent-minded tone, as if he has no idea what this could be about.

The young man clearly points at the woman from behind. That lady noticed him taking photos of the young man, and she let him know. She has gone back to her own table now. She must be telling her husband in her deep bass: 'Night-time New York is full of weirdos...'

'The photos!' repeats the student, without smiling, but there's no aggression in him either. 'Give me your iPhone...'

The man feels as if something's trying to get out of his head, because it's banging from the inside like a hammer.

'Ay-dont-spik-ingleesh-no-anderstend,' he tries to chant, as if reciting a children's poem. His hand is in his coat pocket, holding the iPhone.

But the young man points a finger at the newspaper under the man's arm and says: 'The *New York Times*...'

The man is taken aback.

'Your *New York Times*...' repeats the student, and says something that the man imagines to be: 'You're lying, you can read and speak English, you've bought an American newspaper!', but he doesn't know exactly, because he can't understand English.

'Ay dont spik ingleesh...' he recites by way of a reply.

'You're reading an English newspaper!'

The man decides on a final gesture: he leans forward, bows theatrically to both students and says: 'Aym sori, bai bai.'

He leaves.

No one pursues him.

The café door slams shut and stays that way.

A thought occurs to him, though it's just marginal: 'Why didn't the other student say anything or help his pal?'

The man turns into the nearest side street, something is still banging away in his head like a hammer. He stops, takes out his iPhone and deletes all the photos of the student eating pizza.

When he was little and did something shameful, he was able to wipe it from his mind. He could achieve almost total system shutdown. But he had to go into a trance, by repeating one syllable ad infinitum. Out loud.

So now, as he walks south, away from Times Square, he says to the streets: 'Lalalalalalalalalalalalalalalala...' Or: 'Nananana-nananananananana...'

Night-time New York is full of weirdos.

8

A week ago, three years went by.

The man is lying on a sofa. He likes to read novels set in New York City, and is just finishing the wretched *Goldfinch* by Donna Tartt. Wretched, because the man can't decide if it's a great novel or crap. As soon as he decides it's crap, some golden sentence suddenly pops up in it. He checks online to see what people are saying about it. It's great, they write, and it's crap.

A sentence about a still life has stuck in his mind: 'Whenever you see flies or insects in a still life – a wilted petal, a black spot on the apple – the painter is giving you a secret message.'

What message? Life is death. Everything seems to be full of life, but a small spot marks the beginning of the end, you just have to take a careful look.

There are lots of books from which he remembers just one idea or scene and that's all. It's quite possible that nothing but this still life will remain with him from *The Goldfinch*.

Suddenly, the name 'CD' appears in the novel. The man immediately sees the compact disc he placed in the coffin just before the lid was closed. Beside the left leg, between the calf and the side of the box.

(How greatly he'd impressed the younger man six years earlier!

Not just with this, of course, but it had been a masterful move. Here's what happened:

On the first evening, as they talked, the younger man had dropped the name of a band, Múm, between the lines. It means nothing, and we read it just as we write it. The man knew nothing about it, or any other Icelandic bands with music that's difficult to sing, but he changed the subject without admitting his ignorance. At home, he went straight online: Múm's latest record was available to buy in London for six pounds. The postman delivered it three days later. The next Saturday, when he'd invited the younger man over, the CD was lying on a stack of them next to the hi-fi, as if it had been played many times.

A year later, the man revealed his ploy.

Five years on, he was thrilled to hear the younger man still telling his friends: 'You know, Little Mole really impressed me with that CD...', and then, according to their ritual, the man would add: 'But I've never listened to the whole thing. I've never liked it.')

'The band... just a moment... What was that band called? The band, the Icelandic band...'

He switches off the Kindle.

'Oh my god... I can't remember!'

He whacks himself on the head with his e-reader.

'Noooooo, I can't remember the name of that band! And I was supposed to remember it to the day I die! No one else will know that anymore! The CD is in the grave! Jesus-Christ-I-can't-remember-the-name!'

The man feels ready to burst into tears.

'I was to remember it for ever! And only three years have gone by! What the fuck is that band called?! Ah, got it! MUUUUUMMMMMM, that's it, Múm.'

He puts down the e-reader with Donna Tartt's book, and mindlessly bites his thumb cuticle.

'One day I'll forget! One thousand per cent, I'll forget the name of that band,' he thinks.

'That's what I'm afraid of. That's the very thing.'

9

Three years and ten days later.

An email from his friend (they usually correspond at night – sometimes he sends her a message at three a.m., and when he wakes at ten he finds her answer, sent at five):

'I read that tulips come in all colours – white, pink, red, yellow, purple... every colour except blue. That's exactly what it says: only blue ones aren't there. But K got it into his head that they were blue, I have no idea why. Because they don't exist? Perhaps he didn't know that? Or, on the contrary, he knew, and that's why. Those tulips of his had a faint tinge of pale purple, but really they were blue. (They didn't know they had no right to be...). After a year they faded, and after two they'd gone white.'

LAST WORDS

What should be the closing words of a book by a man of a mature age who loves life, but who thinks about death every day? He thinks about it naturally and with affection. As affectionately as he thinks about life.

The ending of this book came to me on 29 June 2018, on the apron at Warsaw's Chopin Airport, where I was sitting on a plane flying to Sofia.

Do you have the same quirk as I do – that whenever you're about to take off in a plane, you find yourself thinking: 'What if this is my last day on earth?' It always happens to me. Immediately, I mentally run through a list to make sure I've settled life's accounts with everyone and that the people I care about are well disposed towards me. But today my mind prompted me to ask: 'What if the plane crashed, what would be your last words to the world?'

No, it wouldn't be a message to all humanity, like 'Love each other!' I'm not conceited enough.

On the point of death I'd have just two words to say to the world:

'Thank you.'

Bibliography and Useful Links

READING WALLS

Julian Barnes, *Flaubert's Parrot*, Vintage, 2009

Viola Fischerová, *Babí hodina* ('Old Women's Hour'), Nakladatelství Franze Kafky, 1995

Rudolf Matys, 'Jelenka je dítě slunce' ('The deer is a child of the sun') in *Souvislosti* no. 3, 2014, pp. 155–60

Karel Michal, *Everyday Spooks*, translated by David Short, Karolinum Press, 2008

Czesław Miłosz, *Unattainable Earth*, translated by Czesław Miłosz and Robert Hass, Ecco Press, 1986

Radko Šťastný, *Čeští spisovatelé deseti století* ('Czech Writers of Ten Centuries'), SPN, 2001

Jan Zábrana, *Celý život* ('A Whole Life'), Torst, 2001

Works by Viola Fischerová (in Czech): http://www.ipetrov.cz/autor.py/W18

Biography and bibliography of Josef Fischer (in Czech): https://www.phil.muni.cz/fil/scf/komplet/fisjl.html

A HAT FOR THE WORLD

Grzegorz Marzec, *Metafory pamięci* ('Metaphors of Memory'), Instytut Badań Literackich PAN, 2017

A PRESENTIMENT

Websites featuring work by Michał Mroczka:
   https://artinhouse.pl/pl/artysta/michal-mroczka/324
   https://onebid.pl/pl/artist/auctions/Michal-Mroczka
   https://www.behance.net/michalmroczka

A NUMBER OF MANLY SCENES

Tomasz Górnicki's website: https://tomaszgornicki.com

Edi Hila, *Realizm paradoksalny* ('Paradoxical realism'), in *Edi Hila, katalog wystawy* ('Edi Hila: Exhibition Catalogue') at the Museum of Modern Art, Warsaw, 2018 Exhibition website: http://edihila.artmuseum.pl/en/

Dorota Horodyska, 'Saga rodziny Lubonjów, albańskich intelektualistów' ('The saga of the Lubonja family, Albanian intellectuals'), *Wysokie Obcasy* no. 12, 23 March 2002

A STAR AMONG VILLAS

Dorota Leśniak, 'Dom zrehabilitowany' ('A rehabilitated house'), *A&B* no. 3, 2002

Adolf Loos, 'Ornament and crime', https://www2.gwu.edu/~art/Temporary_SL/177/pdfs/Loos.pdf

Vladimír Preclík, *Holomráz*, EVA, 1995

August Sarnitz, *Adolf Loos*, Taschen, 2016

Maria Szadkowska, 'Koncepcja przestrzeni' ('The concept of space'), *A&B* no. 3, 2002

Maria Szadkowska, Martin Polák, Markéta Othová, *Müllerova vila: detaily* ('The Villa Müller: Details'), The City of Prague Museum, 2007

Vladimir Šlapeta, Jana Horneková, Karel Ksandr, Maria Szadkowska, *Müllerova vila v Praze* ('The Villa Müller in Prague'), The City of Prague Museum, 2002

Collective work edited by Karel Ksandr, *Müllerova vila* ('The Villa Müller'), The City of Prague Museum, 2000

Material from the Norbertov Study and Documentation Centre at the City of Prague Museum (Studijní a dokumentační centrum Muzea hlavního města Prahy), https://www.muzeumprahy.cz/en/collections-and-activities-villa-muller-collection/

Website: https://www.muzeumprahy.cz/en/buildings/mullerova-vila-5

THE BOMB OF TIME EXPLODES

Joseph Brodsky, *Less Than One: Selected Essays*, Farrar, Straus & Giroux, 1986

Věra Linhartová, *Prostor k rozlišení* ('Space for Differentiation'), Mladá fronta, 1964

Sándor Márai, *A teljes napló* ('Diary'), Helikon, 2006–18

Władysław Tatarkiewicz, *Historia filozofii* ('History of Philosophy') vol. 2, Wydawnictwo naukowe PWN, 1990.

Krzysztof Varga, *Sonnenberg*, Wydawnictwo Czarne, 2018.

Translator's Afterword

If you've ever been to New York, you may have visited the Museum of Modern Art, and if you did, perhaps you saw sculptures or lithographs by Alexander Calder. His paintings are of simple shapes and squiggles in primary colours, they look effortless, in the 'my five-year-old could do that' category, but they're brilliant and affecting in a way no child's work can be. Whenever I translate Mariusz Szczygieł's writing, I'm reminded of unforced, apparently ingenuous art of this kind. In a few seemingly simple words he tells us a great deal, while also stirring our deepest feelings.

New York is a city that Szczygieł loves and where he often finds inspiration. I was there with him in 2014 to promote *Gottland*, his book about the Czechs, their personality and nationhood. When I went to meet him at the airport, almost the first thing he told me was that he was working on a book about life-changing loss and irreparable absence, and it would be called *Not There*, an idea suggested by his partner. Feeling painfully isolated by the recent death of a close friend, I reacted oversensitively. 'But what do you really know about loss?' I said. A few months later, Szczygieł's partner died unexpectedly, a shattering bolt out of the blue. The project took on a new poignancy and a therapeutic quality; thinking of it as a very personal book, he was surprised by its success, and when in 2019 it won the Nike, Poland's top literary award, it had to be hastily reprinted.

I admire people who can turn traumatic loss into great art, which comforts and fortifies those of us less able to disentangle our own emotions. Szczygieł does confront his own private loss in this book, but the range of stories he has chosen to illustrate his theme shows his extraordinary capacity to find the seeds of profound human experience in tiny details that are nothing to do with him personally (at least not at the outset): a poem on the underground, a banal Excel table, a library book request, a small ad or a box of Christmas tree baubles. In his work each of these unpromising items that most of us would overlook turns out to be the key to a vast hidden world that Szczygieł takes the trouble to explore. And there he finds treasure.

Szczygieł is fascinated by abstract art, whether in the form of painting, sculpture, modernist architecture, poetry or prose, as you can tell from several of the stories in this book. His own writing is equally cryptic, coming up on the main point of the text obliquely, so at first you're not quite sure what you're reading about, but then the picture comes into focus all the more vividly. (The indirect approach also gives the reader licence to see the story from their own viewpoint and form a personal interpretation.) Szczygieł is also fascinated by people, and, with the skills of a disarming interviewer, he's able to get close to his subjects and put them at their ease, drawing out intimate, confessional details that they're happy to entrust to him as an empathetic storyteller. He's an expert at asking the right simple question, and this too can open the door to a new dimension.

As a translator, I think Polish is the ideal language for the economical but powerful writing typical of the Polish school of reportage. The grammatical inflections and flexible word order make it possible to say a lot in a few words, a feature of Polish that I love. But it also makes it challenging to translate – English feels clumsy and verbose by comparison, and as I translate Szczygieł's perfectly balanced sentences I'm trying not to clutter them, but to retain their blithe weightlessness. Each one is like an abstract painting where in three bold brushstrokes the artist conveys an entire frame of mind and triggers a stream of thoughts.

Szczygieł's writing is sometimes very funny, with wordplay that has this translator scratching her head. Interpreting for him before a live audience is nerve-wracking – my brain wonders not just how to translate a witty but risqué remark that already has the Polish spectators laughing, but often whether it's repeatable in polite society. Though it's less unnerving on paper, I worry that here's a case of *not there* – am I getting the joke across? If 'Jerzy Szczygieł in Prague' made you laugh, I've succeeded, but if not... I'm sorry, it's *not there* – something has been lost.

He also uses idiosyncratic idioms that make the translator stop and wonder if they're familiar to most Poles – but they turn out to be Szczygieł's invention. Here, for instance, we have a man too shocked to weep described as *twardy jak luty*, literally 'as hard as February' (though the original meaning of *luty* – February – is 'harsh', 'bleak' or 'cruel', with echoes, to my ear at least, of *lód*, meaning 'ice', and *lutowany*, meaning 'soldered'), and it has a poetic ring (it's two trochees linked by an unstressed syllable); I've put 'as frigid as February', which is all right, but again, perhaps something's *not there*. Yes, even the title of this book, *Nie ma* in Polish, is so unassuming and simple that it defies perfect translation – *nie ma* means 'there isn't' or 'there aren't', a phrase so simple there's no comeback. Full stop. The End. But perhaps in Szczygieł's work it's just the beginning.

Founded in 2023, Linden Editions is dedicated to publishing outstanding literary works of fiction, narrative non-fiction, reportage and essays. These are primarily in translation, from Europe, the Francophonie and the Mediterranean region.

We live and work internationally and enjoy a mixture of cultures, identities and traditions. We intend to use this access to world literature to discover books that merit international exposure: books which tell compelling stories; books which bring fresh, unforgettable voices; and books which are committed, urgent and challenging.

Linden trees grow all over the world, and are often planted at the centre of village squares. People have been gathering under their shade for generations to share stories. Many cultures see the linden tree as sacred, its perfume all-pervading, and its tea curative. Just like the seeds spread by linden trees, we hope our books will spread the seeds of internationalism further.

To discover more, visit lindeneditions.com.

LINDEN TITLES —
PUBLISHED AND OUT SOON

Voracious · Małgorzata Lebda
translated from the Polish by Antonia Lloyd-Jones

In Late Summer · Magdalena Blažević
translated from the Croatian by Anđelka Raguž

Struck · Susanna Bissoli
translated from the Italian by Georgia Wall

Ilaria · Gabriella Zalapi
translated from the French by Adriana Hunter

Milk and Blood · Agnès de Clairville
translated from the French by Frank Wynne